Business Coach Revelations:

Ideas That Many Coaches and Marketing Gurus Won't Tell You

By Ron McIntyre

Ron McIntyre

DISCLAIMER AND/OR LEGAL NOTICES:

Any financial statements or examples are not intended to represent or guarantee that everyone will achieve the same results. Each individual's success will be determined by his or her desire, dedication, effort, and motivation. There are no guarantees you will duplicate the results stated here, you recognize that any business endeavor has inherent risk for loss of capital.

Any reference to any persons or business, whether living or deceased, existing or defunct, is purely coincidental.

PRINTED IN THE USA 2014

Table of Contents

Dedication.. 5

Introduction 6

1. Organize Your Office for Success 8

2. Systematizing and Developing Effective Processes...... 16

3. Profit by Building a T.E.A.M. 31

4. Create Value Add in Your Business & Make 1+1 = 3 48

5. Creating a Powerful Offer.. 56

6. Searching for Immediate Sales.. 63

7. Have Clients that Pay, Stay & Refer!.............................. 77

8. Understand Profit 84

9. Staff Recruitment Training and Development............ 101

10. Profiting from Internet Marketing............................ 124

11. Unlimited Amount of Leads for Your Business?....... 138

12. How to Profit through Time Management 149

So What Do You Do From Here? 178

Dedication

This book is dedicated to the Lord, my wife Toni and my family who have believed in me all these years. I also must remember my first wife Mariellen and Toni's son Christopher who are in heaven watching over us today. It was through their patience and sacrifice of time that I have been able to continue a learning mentality.

This book is made up of practical tips that can help you develop and expand your business with the only limit being your imagination and determination. Because we learn best from repetition, you will find some concepts repeated between chapters for reinforcement. Each chapter can also be read and implemented independently to start with then integrated. I hope you find the chapters helpful and a resource you can return to in time.

"Our greatest weakness lies in giving up. The most certain way to success Is always to try just one more time."
Thomas A. Edison

Introduction

Congratulations for starting on a new journey to improve your small business leadership and marketing skills. By opening this book you have taken the first step in seeing the business world through new eyes.

When I sat at my keyboard to develop the first draft, I found myself with an enormous amount of useful material I've learned and utilized over a number of decades. This experience is drawn from many different business entities including 10 years in multiple roles within retail for well-known chains; ownership and management of my own consulting business; Senior management roles in the IT Consulting world with companies like Covansys and CSC; coaching with John Maxwell Team and development of many website(s). Several of these I continue to own but consult from afar. The strategies I talk about in this book are still in place in many of these companies.

Even though I truly believe we are all 1 or 2 great ideas away from more sales opportunities than we can fully imagine, I believe the first two chapters are as important as the following ten. The strategies in this book - when implemented with intentionality, strategy and care - are guaranteed to make you more money with less effort. These are strategies that have helped businesses just like yours make hundreds of thousands of dollars, possibly including your competitors.

This is the reason I have dedicated my life to Business Consulting and Coaching. Since starting my company to provide direction for small business operators, I have been excited by the demand for coaching, structure, accountability and for the need to have small business operators surrounding themselves with someone that cares and to provide a proper and profitable third party perspective.

As you implement the principles that follow, remember it does not matter what industry or type of business you operate (I've been part of many). What matters is that you grasp the heart and soul of the principles, the underlying lessons and strategies, that can help grow any operation in any category of business imaginable.

We have left the margins wide so one can make notes that are unique to your own company and keep this as a reference point.

The best time to start is NOW, not tomorrow, not next week or next year.

Cheers, Yours in success,

Ron McIntyre

PS. If you would like to arrange a meeting to get a profitable third party perspective on your business, please send an email to ron@transformativeleadership.us and we will gladly arrange a meeting.

1. Organize Your Office for Success

"Have you ever tried to cook a fancy gourmet dinner in a messy, unorganized kitchen?"

It starts out okay. I have all the ingredients I need; it just takes me a little longer to find them as I go. I have to find and clear some counter space, then wipe the crumbs off of it and grab a knife.

Some pots are clean, so I use them first. But then I need the double boiler, and it's still crusted with last night's meal, so I have to wash it. While I'm washing the pot, the garlic and onion that I'm sautéing starts to burn, so I have to run over and rescue it.

Pretty soon, I'm running around like crazy, trying to rescue each item I cook because I'm busy preparing what I need for the next dish. It should be no surprise that the meal was a disaster.

Your place of work is just like that kitchen. It needs to be clean, well-organized, and ready to function to fit your style and personality. Your tools need to be prepared and at the ready in order to support the tasks you and your staff need to complete.

A well set-up office – with all the necessary tools – will save you time and the expense of redundancy. This is the first key to an effective and successful business operation.

Create an Office for Profitability

Most people understand the relationship between time management and profitability. Effective time management increases productivity; more work can be completed in less time, with less distraction and waste.

Office organization also affects profitability and productivity. A tidy and well-structured office is not only a more pleasant place to work, but it also reduces the time anyone might spend looking for items and digging through loose paperwork.

I can't tell you how much time I wasted looking for my glasses on my desk before I adopted this process.

A well-organized office also encourages better internal communication. There are clear areas of the business that are designated for sales news, target tracking, and project planning. This fosters team building and a collaborative work ethic.

Getting Started: Workspace Audit

The best place to start is by taking an honest inventory of the current state of your office or working environment. With that information, you can determine what areas need to be improved, streamlined, or de-cluttered. Spend some time taking a look around your office and note the following:

- Is there a central location where internal company information is displayed?
- What is the distance between your workspace and the printer or photocopier?
- How much loose paper is found around the business?
- What is hung up on the walls? Informative or Distraction?

- Do your staff members have organization systems for their own work areas? Do you provide an example?

- What can be found on your desk?
- How the computers are setup and connected?
- How many files are used on a daily or weekly basis?
- Where are old or outdated files kept?

Organize Your Desk

Presumably, your desk or workstation is where you spend the most time in your office. It is where you are expected to be the most productive. To get all your important tasks completed.

Simply put, you will be more productive and effective if your workspace is clean and organized. Spend some time each day tidying and organizing your workspace – ideally when you are planning your work or your schedule for the following day. It also protects your data from prying eyes.

Here are some other ways you can keep your immediate workspace in the most productive form possible:

Phone. Put your phone on the left side of the desk if you are right handed and on the right side of the desk if you are left handed. Keep a notebook by the phone to record messages and conversation notes. Also record phone messages here, and delete them from your phone system. This seems counter to common sense but it does work.

Personal Items. Keep person items out of your immediate line of sight. Pictures can be distracting, and points for daydreaming.

Organizer. Keep your Daytimer, tablet or Smartphone easily accessible on your desk. Use **one** of these as your main system for appointments, notes, tasks, follow-up, and brainstorming. Keep the rest of your desk clear. I suggest you utilize a well-established software package or online service to record customers, calls, orders etc.? For example, I use a product called IQtell which is a web based GTD system.

Files. Only keep the files you need on your desk or within arm's reach. Store any files you don't use daily or weekly in a filing cabinet further away. Purge files based on a documented aging system.

Inbox and action items. Sort items in your inbox into an easily accessible file sorter or a stack of paper trays. Separate paper into the following categories: to-do, to-review, waiting response, on-hold, to file. Handle requests one time, make decisions the first time you handle request or document. I personally advocate the use of David Allen's Getting Things Done (GTD) Process. Check it out.

Organize Your Office Area

Take the information you gathered in your workplace audit and identify opportunities for improvement. Can the office benefit from a better layout? A paper management system? Sales automation or CRM software? More clearly defined areas? A new filing system?

The answer will depend on the unique needs of your business, and take into account how you and your staff use the space. Here are some suggestions and guidelines for improving the organization of your office or place of business:

Establish Clear Uncluttered Areas

Divide your office into areas of productivity, and locate all related materials and equipment in each area.

Here are some sample areas you may wish to consider:

- Printing and photocopying
- Office supplies
- Financial paperwork and accounting
- Team gathering – Break area
- Kitchen or food-related preparation
- Reception
- Point of sale

Create a Central Location for Information

Many people – including your employees – learn and interpret information that is visual, better than any other means of communication, i.e. auditory or tactile. A central location in your office for staff to go for company information and updates is an essential tool for team building and internal communications.

Now we can move into a section I like to refer to as **"What Every Office Needs!"**

Tools Every Office Needs

Whiteboard

Place a whiteboard in an easily accessed place – your staff communication center, conference room or the boardroom. This whiteboard is for brainstorming, project planning, marketing planning, or any other use that may be required.

This is a great tool for team meetings, client meetings, and management meetings. The facilitator can diagram information and work through issues on the spot.

If your work relies heavily on virtual meetings and conversations then I would ensure that your conference package includes the "whiteboard" concept within the offering. Could be something as simple as Google+.

Sales Status Board

Create a customized sales status board for your business. Take a whiteboard, and some thin black tape, and create a chart or diagram that records regular sales statistics and targets. You may be able to find one that is already sectioned off into grids for easy adaptation.

You may wish to separate the whiteboard into two sections – target sales and actual sales, and compare based on weekly, quarterly, and yearly targets. You can also compare actual sales to budgeted sales for the same period the previous year.

12-Month Marketing Planner

Chart your marketing plan on a large calendar and post it in a central area. This is a clear reminder of the big picture, and each of the promotions you have planned over the course of the year.

Remember to write in dry-erase marker so you can easily make changes. Consider color-coding your promotions or projects for easy visibility. Also recondition any whiteboards on a regular basis so they last longer.

Manage Paper + Filing

System	Steps
Create a master filing system and color code it	Group vendor files (AP) and assign a color Group client files (AR) and assign a color Group project or product files
Sort each filing category by date or alphabetically by name	Sort vendor or supplier files by name Sort client files by client number or name Sort project files by project number or name
Create a binder of master lists for regularly accessed information **(Security is Critical)**	Office passwords Financial accounts Goals Birthdays Vendor contact information

Use a bound notebook	Keep track of phone calls and messages Put the date on each page Eliminate loose notepaper Automate when possible
Get rid of magazines **Keep materials selectively**	Throw away industry magazines and newspapers Keep relevant articles of interest Sort them into files, if necessary
Keep tax-related documents in one spot	File all receipts, donations and other tax related information in the same filing cabinet Make copies of documents you need to file in more than one spot or automate receipt capture
Create a business care management system	Throw away old business cards Organize cards by last name or company name in a binder, rolodex or automated business card capture Enter the information in a data management program, then throw away the cards

2. Systematizing and Developing Effective Processes

"One of the biggest mistakes a business owner can make is to create a company that is dependent on the owner's involvement for the success of its daily operations."

This is called working "in" your business. You're writing basic sales letters, licking stamps, and guiding staff step-by-step through each task.

There are a number of problems with this approach. One is redundancy. You're paying your staff to carry out tasks that you eventually complete. The second is poor time management. You're spending your day – at your high hourly rate – on tasks as they arise, leaving little room for the tasks you need to be focused on.

However, the biggest issue I have with this approach is that countless intelligent business owners are spending the majority of their time operating their business, instead of **growing** it.

A good test of this is to ask yourself, what would happen if you took off to a hot sunny destination for three weeks and left your Smart phone and laptop/tablet at home. Would your business be able to continue operating?

If you said no, then this chapter is for you.

Systematizing your business is about putting policies and procedures in place to make your business operations run smoother – and more importantly – without your constant involvement. It's about empowering your people and encouraging a culture of accountability. With your newfound free time, **you will be able to focus your efforts** on the bigger picture: strategically growing your business.

Why Systematize?

For most small business owners, systems simply mean freedom from the day-to-day functioning of their organization. The company runs smoothly, makes a profit, and provides a high level of service – regardless of the owner's involvement.

Systematizing your business is also a healthy way to plan for the future. You're not going to be working forever – what happens when you retire? How will you transition your business to new ownership or management? How will you take that vacation you've been dreaming of?

Businesses that function without their owners being hands-on are also highly valuable to investors. Systematizing your business can position it in a favorable light for purchase, and merit a higher price tag.

A system is any process, policy, or procedure that consistently achieves the same result, regardless of who is completing the task.

Any task that is performed in your business more than once can be systematized. Ideally, the tasks that are completed on a cyclical basis – daily, weekly, monthly, and quarterly – should be systematized so much so that anyone can perform them.

Systems can take many forms – from manuals and instruction sheets, to signs, banners, audio or video recordings and software package installations. They don't have to be elaborate or extensive, just provide enough information in step-by-step form to guide the person performing the task.

Benefits of Business Systems (Processes)

There are virtually unlimited benefits available to you and your business through systemization. The more systems you can successfully implement, the more benefits you'll see:

- Better cost management
- Improved time management
- Clearer expectations of staff, happier employees
- Increased employee engagement
- More effective staff training and orientation
- Increased productivity (and potentially profits)
- Happier customers (consistent service)
- Maximized conversion rates
- Increased staff respect for your time
- Increased level of individual initiative
- Greater focus on long-term business growth

Taking Stock of Your Existing Systems

The first step in systematizing your business is taking a long look at the existing systems (if any) in your business. At this point, you can look for any systems that have simply emerged as "the way we do things here."

How does your staff answer the phone? What is the process customers go through when dealing with your business? How are employees hired? Trained? How is performance Reviewed and rewarded?

Some of your systems may be highly effective, and not require any changes. Others may be ineffective and require reworking or replacement. If you have previously established some systems, now is a good time to check-in and evaluate how well they are functioning.

Use the following chart to record what systems currently exist in your business.

	Existing Systems
Administration	
Financial	
Communication	

Customer Relations	
Employees	
Marketing	

Seven Suggested Areas to Systematize

There is no doubt that system creation – especially when none exist to begin with – is a daunting and time-consuming task. For many businesses, it can be difficult to determine where to start to make the best use of their time from the onset.

Here are seven main areas of your business you focus on to Systematize. Begin with one area, and move to the other areas as you are ready. Alternately, start with one or two systems within each area, and evaluate how those new systems affect your business. Each business will require its own unique set of systems.

1. Administration

This is an important area of your business to Systematize because administrative roles tend to see a high turnover. A series of systems will reduce training time, and keep you from explaining how the phones are to be answered each time a new receptionist joins your team.

Administrative Systems	
Opening and closing procedures	Filing and paper management
Phone greeting	Workflow
Mail processing	Document production
Shipping/mailing procedures	Inventory management
Office maintenance (watering plants, emptying recycle bins, etc.)	Order processing
	Making orders

2. Financial

This is one area of systems that you will need to keep a close eye on – but that doesn't mean you have to do the work yourself. Financial management systems are everything from tracking credit card purchases to invoicing clients and following up on overdue accounts. Don't forget to look at automated options with audit capability by a local accountant.

These systems will help to prevent employee theft, and allow you to always have a clear picture of your numbers. It will allow you to control purchasing, and ensure that each decision is signed-off on.

I highly recommend small businesses look at off-the-shelf software, software-as-a-service or local professionals to simplify this area.

Financial Systems	
Purchasing	Profit / loss statements
Credit card purchase tracking	Invoicing
Accounts payable	Daily cash out
Accounts receivable	Petty cash
Bank deposits	Employee expenses
Cutting checks	Payroll
Tax payments	Commission payments

3. Communications

The area of communication is essential and time consuming for any business. Fax & email templates, sales letters, internal memos, reports, and automated newsletters are items that need to be created regularly by different people in your organization.

Most of the time, these communications aren't much different from one to the next, yet each are created from scratch by a different person. There is a huge opportunity for systemization in this area of your business. Systematized communication ensures consistency and company differentiation.

Communication Systems	
Internal memo template	Newsletter template
Fax & email templates	Sales letter template(s)
Letterhead template	Meeting minutes template
Team meeting agenda	Report template
Sending faxes & emails	Internal meetings
Internal emails	Scheduling

4. Customer Relations

Another important area for systemization is customer relations. This includes everything the customer sees or touches in your company, as well as any interaction they might have with you or your staff members.

Establishing a customer relations system will also ensure that new staff members understand how customers are handled in *your* business. It will allow you to maintain a high level of customer service, without constantly reminding staff of your policies. It will also ensure that the success of your customer relations and retention does not hinge on you or any other individual salesperson.

Customer Relations Systems (CRM)	
Incoming phone call script	Sales process
Outgoing phone call script	Sales script
Customer service standards	Newsletter templates
Customer retention strategy	Ongoing customer communication strategy
Customer communications templates	Customer liaison policy

5. Employees

Create systems in your business for hiring, training, and developing your employees. This will establish clear expectations for the employee, and streamline time consuming activities like recruitment.

Employees with clear expectations who work within clear structures are happier and more productive. They are motivated to be more engaged when they know they will be recognized if they meet or exceed expectations. Establishing a clear training manual will also save you and your staff the time and hassle of training each new staff member on the fly.

Employee Systems	
Employee recruitment	Staff uniforms or dress code
Employee retention	Employee training
Incentive and rewards program	Ongoing training and professional development
Regular employee reviews	Job descriptions and role profiles
Employee feedback structure	

6. Marketing

This is likely an area in which you spend a large part of your time. Your focus should be on generating new leads and getting more people to call you or walk through your doors. These efforts can be systematized and delegated to other staff members.

Use the information in this program to create simple systems for your basic promotional efforts. Any one of your staff should be able to pick up a marketing manual and implement a successful direct mail campaign or place a purposeful advertisement.

Marketing Systems	
Referral program	Regular advertisements
Customer retention program	Advertisement creation system
Regular promotions	Direct mail system
Marketing calendar	Sales procedures

Enquiries management	Lead management

7. Data

While we like to think we operate a paperless office, often the opposite is true. Your business needs to have clear systems for managing paper and electronic information to ensure that information is protected, easily accessed, and only kept when necessary.

Data management systems help you keep your office organized. Everyone knows where information is to be stored, and how it is to be handled, which prevents big stacks of paper with no place to go.

Understand your customer's desire and need for privacy, confidentiality and respect, this is critical.

Ensure that within your data management systems you include a data backup system. That way, if anything happens to you server or computer software, your data – and potentially your business – is protected. Seek help to develop a Business Recovery program in the remote event of a catastrophic situation.

Data Management Systems	
IT Management	Client file system
Data backup	Project file system
Computer repairs	Point of sale system
Electronic information storage	Financial data management

Implementing New Systems

If you completed the exercise earlier in this chapter, you will have a good idea of the systems that are currently in place in your business. The next step is to determine what systems you need to create in your business.

To do this you will need to get a better understanding of the tasks that you and your employees complete on a daily and weekly basis. If you operate a timesheet program, this can be a good source of information. Alternately, ask staff to keep a daily log for a week of all the tasks they contribute to or complete. Doing so will not only give you valuable insight into their how they spend their time on a daily basis, but also involve them in the Systematizing process.

Review all task logs or timesheet records at the end of the week, remove duplicates, and group like tasks together. From here you can categorize the tasks into business areas like the seven listed above, or create your own categories.

Then, you will need to prioritize and plan your system creation and implementation efforts. Choose one from each category, or one category to focus on at a time. The amount you can take on will depend on your business needs, and the staff resources you have available to you for this process.

Determine if there is an automated alternative that is cost effective and more reliable. If not then begin developing your new systems. Remember that system creation is a long-term process – not something that will transform your business overnight. Be patient, and focus on the items that hold the highest priority.

Creating Your Systems

There is a big variety of ways you can create systems for your business – depending on the type of system you need and the type of business you operate. Some systems will be short and simple – i.e., a laminated sign in the kitchen that outlines step-by-step how to make the coffee – while others will be more complex – i.e., your sales scripts or letter templates.

One thing all of your systems have in common is steps. There is a linear process involved from start to finish. Begin by writing out each of the steps involved in completing the task, and provide as much detail as you can.

Then, review your step-by-step guide with the employee(s) who regularly complete the task and gather their feedback. Once you have incorporated their input, decide what format the system needs to be in: automated, manual, laminated instruction sheet, sign, office memo, etc.

Testing Your Systems – Critical Step

Now that you have created or purchased a system, you will need to make sure that it works. More specifically, you need to make sure that it works without your involvement.

Implement the new system for an appropriate period of time – a week or month – then ask for input from staff, suppliers and vendors, and customers. Evaluate if it is informative enough for your staff, seamless enough for your suppliers, and whether or not it meets or exceeds your customer's needs.

Take that feedback and revise the system accordingly. You will rarely get the system right the first time – so be patient.

Systems will also need to be evaluated and revised on a regular basis to ensure your business processes are kept up to date. Structure an annual or bi-annual review of systems, and stick to it.

Employee Buy-In & Adoption

It will be nearly impossible for you to develop effective systems without the involvement and input of your employees. These are the people who will be using the systems, and who are completing the tasks on a regular basis without systems. They have a wealth of knowledge to assist you in this process.

Employees can also draft the systems for you to review and finalize. This will make the systemization process a much faster and more efficient one.

It is also important to note that when you introduce new systems into your company, there may be a natural resistance to the change. People – including your employees – are habitual people who can become set in the way they are used to doing things. Look for agreement or resistance when dealing with breakup of comfort zones.

Delegation

The final step to Systematizing your business is delegation. What is the point of creating systems unless someone other than you can use them to perform tasks?

This doesn't have to mean completely removing your involvement from the process, but it does mean giving your employees enough freedom to complete the task within the structure of the systems you have spent time and considerable thought creating. Allow your employees the possibility of temporary failure and fresh start up with new alternatives. After that, allow yourself the freedom of focusing on the tasks that you most enjoy, and most deserve your time – like creating big picture strategies to grow your business and increase your profits.

John Maxwell spends a fair amount of time in his books defining delegation and its importance to your growth as a leader. I highly suggest you locate a coach to help you fully develop this part of your leadership practice.

3. Profit by Building a T.E.A.M.

"The acronym T.E.A.M. simply means Together Everyone Accomplishes More!"

The people you employ contribute – directly or indirectly – on a daily basis to the strength and vitality of your business. You can't run your business alone, so you rely on their skills and support. In simpler words, your employees help you to make money.

But your employees are not just the people who arrive at your office every day and exchange effort for a paycheck. Their role is not just to build capacity and sell more or serve more.

Your employees are part of a potentially powerful group of people that you can leverage to put your business on the fast track to success. Your staff is more than the people who work for you. They are actually members of your team – the group of people who are collectively working to achieve the same objective, or reach the same vision.

I say they are more than just employees because their collective, cohesive value is actually much higher than their individual worth.

We all know that more people working on the same task will ensure the task is completed faster. In business, when you have more people working together on the same task, you save time, increase brainpower, and ultimately, **make more money**.

Corporate Culture

Corporate Culture has become a common buzzword when it comes to building a successful business, and rightly so.

Your corporate culture is the environment in which you run your business, and the environment in which your team members work. It is rooted in the vision, mission, values and beliefs of the organization, and dictates the "kind of office" and "kind of people" that work in that office.

Corporate culture is something that typically develops organically. The business owner and senior employees create a positive or negative environment based solely on who they are as people and how they behave as leaders. You simply can't avoid creating some type of corporate culture when you run a business.

You can, however, avoid creating a negative or unproductive corporate culture. Whether you are just starting out, or seeking to improve your workplace, you do have control over the type of environment in which you run your business.

Like most things in business, this won't happen overnight. However, with a clear idea of your values, where you want to go, and what you want to create, you'll be well on your way to getting there.

Vision

Your company's vision statement should be a brief, bold, and clear sentence that every one of your employees knows and understands. It is a roadmap to your idea of success; if you don't know what that looks like, how will you know when you achieve it?

If your goal is to create a highly profitable company – what does highly profitable mean? $1 million in annual sales? $3 million in annual profit?

Do you seek to become the industry leader in sprocket production? How will this be measured? How many sprockets will you have to produce to reach this goal? What is the long term potential of your product in the market?

The vision statement is a short summary of the long-term objective of the company. What the company will look like, produce, achieve; it is how you know the company is "successful."

Many companies either do not have a vision statement or they keep it a secret from their employees. It is only discussed in board meetings or management meetings. For a team to collectively work toward a goal, they need to know what the big picture objective is. They need to have a personal buy-in with the company's direction, and they expect to be communicated with on a regular basis.

Be proud of your vision. Keep it visible for staff – post it on the wall, include it in internal communications, and connect day to day activities too it as often as possible.

Creating a Vision Statement

The process of creating a vision statement is something that you can work through alone, or in collaboration with your team. It is highly recommended to review the draft vision statement with your employees to ensure they understand and support the goals and objectives of the company.

Keep the following points in mind when crafting your vision statement:

- **Think big** – Why did you start or buy this business? What was your dream or purpose in doing so?
- **Think long-term** – Vision statements should last five to 10 or even 25 years but review it on a regular basis. Don't lock it in a desk drawer.
- **Be specific** – Use numbers, dates, ratings systems

and other ways of measuring success

- **Be succinct** – Use clear, short, simple sentences that are easy to repeat and remember

Mission

Your mission statement is a general description of how you are going to achieve your vision. This is a longer and more detailed statement that should include what your business is, who your customers are, and how you are different from (better than!) the competition. Do you have a unique differentiator?

Creating Your Mission Statement:

Here is a recommended process for completing your mission statement:

Step One: List your company's core strengths and weaknesses; what do you do well? What do you need to work on, or avoid doing?

Step Two: Who are your primary customers? Describe the types of customers you serve – both internal and external.

Step Three: What do your customers think of your strengths? What strengths are most important to them? Go ahead and ask them if you need to.

Step Four: Connect the strength that each customer values with its customer type. Write it in a sentence. Combine any redundancies.

Step Five: Organize your sentences in order of importance

Step Six: Combine your sentences into a paragraph

or two. Elaborate on points as needed. This is your draft mission statement.

Step Seven: Consult with your staff and customers, and ask for their feedback. Do employees support the statement? Can they act on it? Do customers want to do business with a company with this mission statement? Does it make sense?

Step Eight: Incorporate the feedback received, and refine the statement until you are happy with it. Then publish it – everywhere.

Culture or Values Statements

Your culture or values statement is the next step in the process. It describes how you and your staff will act when taking action (your mission statement) to achieve your objective (your vision statement).

Much like every family has their own belief system and way of doing things – from cooking to cleaning to raising kids – every company has their own set of values when it comes to running a business. It reflects the unique personality of the organization.

Creating Your Culture Statement

Involve your team in creating your company's culture or values statement. Generally, this is a point-form document that reflects the beliefs of the company, its employees, and its customers.

It can be helpful to think about the type of people you currently employ, as well as the ones you may wish to employ. What are they like? What are their belief systems? What are their most important values? The values should be lived and reflected by every member of your company.

Remember that the culture or values statement is usually the longest of the three statements – and that's okay.

Sample Vision, Mission & Cultural Statements

Sample Vision Statements

Here are some real examples of corporate vision statements:

"At Microsoft, our mission and values are to help people and businesses through the world realize their potential." – Microsoft

"To be the company that best understands and satisfies the product, service and self-fulfillment needs of women - globally." - Avon

"Our vision is to be earth's most customer centric company; to build a place where people can come to find and discover anything they might want to buy online." – Amazon

Sample Mission Statements

"The Mission of McGill University is the advancement of learning through teaching, scholarship and service to society: by offering to outstanding undergraduate and graduate students the best education available; by carrying out scholarly activities judged to be excellent when measured against the highest international standards; and by providing service to society in those ways for which we are well-suited by virtue of our academic strengths." – McGill University, Montreal, Canada

"Starbucks purchases and roasts high-quality whole bean coffees and sells them along with fresh, rich-brewed, Italian style espresso beverages, a variety of pastries and confections, and coffee-related accessories and equipment -

- primarily through its company-operated retail stores. In addition to sales through our company-operated retail stores, Starbucks sells whole bean coffees through a specialty sales group and supermarkets. Additionally, Starbucks produces and sells bottled Frappuccino® coffee drink and a line of premium ice creams through its joint venture partnerships and offers a line of innovative premium teas produced by its wholly owned subsidiary, Tazo Tea Company. The Company's objective is to establish Starbucks as the most recognized and respected brand in the world." – Starbucks

Sample Culture Statement

Our Culture

Values-based leadership. Our Credo outlines the values that provide the foundation of how we act as a corporation and as individual employees so that we continue to put the needs of the people we serve first.

Diversity. It's our individual differences that make us stronger as a whole. We recognize the strength and value that comes when collaborative relationships are built between people of different ages, race, gender, religion, nationality, sexual orientation, physical ability, thinking style, personal backgrounds and all other attributes that make each person unique.

Innovation. True innovation can only be fostered within a supportive environment that values calculated risk in order to achieve the maximum reward. At Johnson & Johnson Inc., we encourage and reward innovative thinking, innovative solutions and an innovative approach in all that we do.

Passion. The deep desire to enrich people's lives – by delivering quality products and remarkable experiences that *make their lives easier, healthier and more joyful.*

Collaboration. *The unwavering belief that great results depend on the ability to create trusting relationships.*

Courage. *The fearless pursuit of the unproven, unknown possibility – the willingness to take great risks for the benefit of the greater good.*

- Johnson & Johnson Canada

Communications

The only way to build and maintain a strong team is through strong, consistent communication. This is often an overlooked or neglected aspect of business management, and is easily forgotten during periods of high stress or heavy workload.

Avoid letting communication fall on the backburner by creating a meaningful regular meeting schedule – and sticking to it. Depending on the size and type of your business, daily, weekly, or monthly team meetings are an important cornerstone of a strong team.

Regularly scheduled team meetings are like Sunday dinners with a busy family. They give you – the owner – a regular forum with your staff to implement company-wide training initiatives, announce results, establish goals and targets, or share new visions or directions. They also give your staff a forum to share feedback and air grievances. Give your staff permission to be open and honest in their discussions.

Dynamic Meeting Framework – Critical Activity

By now you're probably thinking, "Sure, I hear some company's regular team meetings are effective, but we tried them and it didn't work," or "I held regular team meetings, but after a while, no one showed up."

There is a difference between team meetings held for the sake of having team meetings, and well prepared team meetings with a purpose.

You need to start holding team meetings with a purpose.

Know Your Purpose

Each team meeting should have a purpose and clear objectives. Is it to educate? Build consensus? Gather feedback?

Once you have established a purpose for a particular meeting, send an agenda to your staff confirming the meeting and outlining your objectives. This is a good time to ask if anyone has a subject they would like to raise at the meeting.

If you find you do not have a clear purpose or objective, ask yourself if a team meeting is the best use of time for that week and consider postponing it to the next regularly scheduled time slot.

Establish a Schedule That Everyone Can Commit To

Scheduling is potentially the biggest challenge when trying to set up a team meeting. Often, all of your staff members are busy going in eight different directions to fulfill their roles and operating on dramatically different schedules.

This is one reason why regular team meetings are important. Ad hoc meetings require ad hoc scheduling, and reduce the likelihood that all your team members will be able to attend.

Ask your team to block off one hour (or two) each week (or month) for the team meeting in a time slot that is convenient for everyone. Establish a clear attendance expectation from everyone. This will exclude that time slot from the scheduling of other meetings and avoid conflict.

If you find that a team meeting is not necessary one week, you can always cancel it. Don't hold a meeting because you always have one, make sure there is a purpose or need.

Plan Each and Every Minute

The biggest complaint from employees about team meetings is the length. Too often team meetings run out of control, and end up taking three hours instead of one. You will quickly lose team focus and respect for the regular meeting this way. By establishing a clear agenda and staying on topic, you can run an efficient, succinct meeting.

Your detailed agenda should include:

- meeting purpose or objective
- list of topics and associated speakers
- list of decisions that need to be made/agreed to
- time allocation for each topic
- opportunity for additional topics at the end

Circulate your draft agenda in advance of the meeting, and request input and feedback. When all team members have reviewed and contributed to the agenda, you will increase their level of ownership and buy-in into the process.

Establish the Facilitator

Choose one person to chair the meeting and keep it on track. This is generally the business owner or a senior member of the team with some authority over junior staff and a high level of respect.

It is the responsibility of the facilitator – or chairperson – to create an environment of open dialogue and trust, and to keep the meeting on schedule.

Create a Follow-up Schedule

Assign the task of taking detailed meeting minutes to a team member – or rotate this responsibility on a regular basis. It is important to record what happens in team meetings, just as you would in a client-related business meeting.

In the minutes, establish a system for tracking the action items that arise from decisions made in the meeting. This can be set up as a simple chart:

Decision	Action	Responsibility	Deadline

Make sure that these responsibilities are assigned and agreed upon in the meeting, and clear deadlines are established. Reviewing or following up on this chart can serve as a regular topic during team meetings.

Circulate meeting minutes to all attendees and ask for input or revisions. You may wish to circulate meeting minutes with the agenda for the next team meeting, and gather feedback at the same time.

Motivations + Incentives for Team Building

A big challenge in team building is coming up with new ways to foster and maintain a high level of motivation. How do you keep teams of people excited and driven to succeed over long periods of time? How do you keep your team motivated to improve their performance, and increase their achievements?

It is important to note that we're not just talking about individuals, but teams of people working together. It is fairly simple to motivate a single person, but an entire team of motivated people will generate significantly higher results.

The key here is to give incentives for individual and team accomplishments. Incentives that reward based on collective achievement require people to work together and motivate each other to succeed.

Before we start talking about monetary and incentive-based rewards, it's important to look at motivational factors that are not incentive-driven.

Give People Room to Work – Get out of the way!

Employees who feel their managers and supervisors believe and trusts in their abilities are happier and will always perform at a higher level than those who do not. They are motivated to "prove them right" and feel supported in their efforts.

Micromanagement quickly reduces morale. It is essential that you and your managers clearly express confidence in your team members. You hired them to do a job, perform a role, so you must ensure they have the space and permission to do so.

When you put effective systems in place and establish clear expectations, you create a clear context or boundary system for employees to work within. They understand the decision-making hierarchy, and the general way 'things are done around here.'

Your team should be encouraged to take initiative and to take risks within this context. You have hired your team based on their skills and intellectual capabilities, and thus should be able to trust in their choices and decision making abilities.

There is Value in Incentives

Incentives are great motivators. An incentive is a reason to perform or act in a certain way. For example, if your team increases sales by 40% by month's end, they will be treated to an expensive dinner.

Incentives need to be specific and have deadlines in order to be effective. In the example above, sales need to increase by 40% by the end of the month in order for the team to receive their dinner. If sales only increase by 30%, or if they increase by 40% at the end of the second month, the team does not earn their reward.

Time-specific incentives increase the sense of urgency, and encourage staff to work harder to achieve the objective. If the incentive is not time-bound, there is no reason to work faster or harder, since staff will assume they will reach their milestone "eventually."

Rarity is also a key component of effective incentive-based team building. If the reward is ongoing (i.e., if staff receive an expensive dinner every month sales are over $75,000), then "there's always next time." There is a lesser incentive to push performance to receive the reward. Some team members may care one month, but not the next.

Monetary Incentives

Bonuses and salary increases are a popular way to give your team an incentive to perform. Not always the most effective yet popular.

These can include:

- · Commissions

- · Bonuses for completing a challenging project, or hitting a jointly agreed target

- · Rewards for highest producing employee

- · Salary increases based on met measurable targets

It's up to you how you choose to structure your monetary incentives, based on your budget and resources. Remember to ensure that the terms of each incentive are clearly outlined, and that both parties (you and your employee) understand the agreement.

Special Gift Rewards

Physical, tangible gifts are an inexpensive way to reward your team for achievements and improvement. These rewards show that you have given some level of thought to what they might enjoy or appreciate in exchange for a job well done. They're also a great way to surprise employees.

Here are some ideas:

- Spa gift certificates
- Books – *consider motivational or business-related topics*
- CDs or DVDs
- Meals – lunch or breakfast

- Other gift certificates – gas, food, meals, local shops
- Movie or theater tickets
- Weekend getaway – hotel, meals, etc.
- Flowers
- Gym memberships

Your Team Leaders

The strength of a team lies in the strength of the people who lead it. No group of people is effective without strong leadership, just like no business is effective without a strong owner or management team. The key to positive employee engagement lies in well trained and motivated leaders.

Building a strong team means knowing who your leaders are – both in job description and natural ability.

Understanding the strength of your natural leaders and the skills of your natural followers will allow you to strategically structure your team for maximum effectiveness and efficiency. It will give you insight into who is best suited for management promotions and project management; which team members have the ability to assemble and motivate their peers.

Your leaders need to have a high degree of passion for your product or service, and truly believe in the company's vision. They need to be able to handle a high level of responsibility, and manage a range of people to achieve a common goal.

Your leaders are your team builders. They present new ideas, build consensus, and encourage the involvement of others.

Types of Leaders

Simply speaking, there are basically four main types, or styles, of leaders. Chances are you've experienced each type at some point in your career. What type do you exhibit and what types do you encourage in your company?

Type	Description	Ideal Use
Autocratic	Classical or "old-school" approach Manager holds all power and decision-making authority No employee consultation or input Orders are obeyed Rewards/punishment structure	New, untrained employees Detailed orders and instructions are required No other leadership style has been effective Limited time available Department restructuring High production requirements
Bureaucratic	"By the book" approach All is done to specific procedures/policies All tasks outside policies referred to higher management	Routine tasks performed Standards and procedures need to be communicated regularly Safety or training Cash handling

Laissez-faire	"Hands-off" approach Employees have almost total freedom Little direction or guidance is provided Employees must make own decisions, set own goals Employees must solve own problems	Highly skilled and experienced employees Employees are highly driven and ambitious Consultants are being managed Employees are trustworthy
Democratic	"Participatory approach" Employees part of decision making process Employees well informed Leader has final say, but involved others Collaborative approach Encourages employee development with guidance and assistance from leader Leader recognizes and rewards achievement	Collaborative environment Employee development and growth is the focus Changes or problems affect employees and require their input to create a solution Team building and participation is encouraged

4. Create Value Add in Your Business & Make 1+1 = 3

"What happens when demand for your products or services slows or stops? What happens when the competition sets up shop with a "new and improved" version of your product down the road?"

The majority of small businesses, like yours, are established in response to market demand for a product or service. Many build their businesses by serving that demand, and enjoy growing profits without putting much effort into long-term planning or marketing.

How do you keep your offering fresh, while growing and maintaining your client base? The answer is by adding value to your product or service.

Added value is a marketing or customer relations strategy that can take the form of a product or service, which is added to the original offering for free, or as part of a discounted package. It, like all other elements in your marketing toolkit, is designed to attract new customers and retain existing ones. A simple example of added value would be if you owned a gift shop, and offered complimentary gift wrapping with every purchase.

If you don't refresh and renew your offering over time, your customers will get bored and be drawn to your competitor. Your employees, too, may become disinterested, and find work elsewhere. Ultimately, both clients and employees will demand additional value to remain loyal – and aren't they the keystones for your business growth?

Can You Add Value to Your Business?

Everyone can add value to their business. More accurately, everyone can *afford* to add value to their business. Adding value doesn't have to blow your marketing budget, or take up hours of your time. There are many ways – big and small – to enhance your business in the eyes of your clients.

The key to adding value is determining what your customers and target market perceive as valuable. You must understand their needs, wants, troubles and inconveniences in order to entice them with solutions through added value products or services. Adding value will add to your profits, but if you don't focus on genuinely helping your clients, you'll have a difficult time attracting them. What kind of experience do they want?

Added value works for both product and service based businesses. If you offer a service, like hairstyling, try treating your customers with products like a latte while they wait, shampoo samples, or a free conditioning treatment with every sixth visit. If you sell a product, consider offering convenience services – like free shipping or delivery – to make the customer's experience a seamless one. The customer will feel appreciated and their needs will have been taken care of.

Ways to Add Value to Your Business

There are many ways to enhance your offer, depending on your budget and the resources you have access to. You may wish to hold a brainstorming session with your staff to come up with ideas for your business; if your employees are on the front lines, they'll likely have firsthand information about what clients would like to see more of.

Feature Your Expertise

Your intellectual property is a free resource that you have at your disposal to share with your clients. This will make them feel as though they have an inside track. You might want to consider adding it to your business, making it a value-added service.

Expert corner: Supplement your website and newsletter with columns on topics of interest to your customers and of relevance to your service. This will position you as an expert in the marketplace, and give your clients helpful information they won't receive from the competition.

Do It Yourself Tips: This is a great tool for seasonal marketing. Provide your clients with this information on your website, in your newsletters, or on take away note cards in your store or office. Ideas include recipes, craft ideas, gift ideas – all of which are branded with your company logo and contact information, and include your product as an ingredient.

What to Expect Tips: Take your customer through what they should expect in the first few days (weeks) of using your service or product, and how they can make the most of it. This can include assembly instructions, product care and cleaning, or service results (like a 25% increase in business – guaranteed!).

Related + Community Events: Own a store that sells athletic equipment? Post information on your website, in store, and in your newsletter about upcoming races, games, or consumer trade shows. Or simply keep a bulletin in your office of community events and offers that will draw your clients in, and establish itself as a hub in the neighborhood for information.

Offer Convenience Services:

Customer service is a dying practice in our high paced culture – use it to your advantage. When done well, it can be the difference between you and the competition, or the deciding factor for a potential repeat client.

Envision the steps involved for a customer to arrive at your store, purchase your offering, and use your product or service. Can you eliminate any of those steps for them? Can you shorten waiting times, or make them more pleasurable? Stepping into your clients' shoes will allow you to determine the most powerful value add for your company. Here are a few ideas:

Free Delivery + Shipping: With clearly established parameters (will you ship your product free to India?); this is a solid value added service that many businesses offer. Free delivery (usually with a purchase over a set amount) is a huge convenience for many people who do not have access to a vehicle, or need help moving large items.

Follow up Services: This works great for computers, appliances and other mechanical or technology-based products. Offer maintenance and service contracts for three time periods; instead of dealing with the manufacturer, customers will rely on you for assistance which brings them back into the store and establishes a relationship of trust.

Remember, the delivery of the product or service does not end your relationship, be sure to follow-up post-delivery and provide some level of support or contact.

Gift-Wrapping: A great service to provide – especially for seasonal gifts. This service costs very little, and can have a big impact on your customer's experience.

"While You Wait" Amenities: If you could make your customer feel like a VIP for minimal cost, why wouldn't you? Offering amenities like coffee and treats, free samples and services (wireless Internet is a big one) will go a long way.

Comparison-Shopping Tools: Show your customers that you are so sure your product will measure up against the competition that you'll help them compare.

Establish Complementary Partnerships:

Complementary partnerships with other businesses can take you a long way toward adding value for your customer, and generating new business. Just like a joint testimonial mailing, the power (and convenience) of referral business is immense.

Build a web of associates: If you're a yoga instructor, carry the cards of your treatment providers (physiotherapists, massage therapists, etc.) to refer your students to. In exchange, your brochure or card is posted in their offices. This works for automotive repair, esthetics, consultants and other service providers. Customers will trust referrals received by their existing service providers, and feel taken care of by a reputable community of experts.

Establish partnerships with financial incentives: This is one that has your interests in mind as well as your customers'. In addition to establishing a complementary partnership with a related associate, establish an incentive structure where each of you is compensated for your referrals. For example, if you refer a client to a furniture store after they've purchased a mattress from you, and they buy a bed frame, your associate will pay you a portion of the sale – and vice versa.

Location-based partnerships: Consider creating partnerships with the businesses around you – even if your products and services don't appear to be related. Shopping malls do this all the time with value coupon books that customers must purchase for $5 to $20 dollars. These partnerships and incentives will keep the customer spending money in the area, which is good for everyone's bottom line.

Packages + Bundles

Packaging and bundling products and services is one of the most popular methods of adding value. Clients perceive the bundles as having a higher value than the sum of the individual items – or as receiving something for free.

Cleverly packaged and named bundles can spark interest and revive your products in the eyes of your customers. Remember to always give the offers an end date or provide a limited number to create a sense of scarcity and urgency and to prevent this strategy from going stale.

Intuitive product bundles: Package independent related products together, and give them a reduced price or name. For example, this could be selling an extra pair of running socks with new running shoes. Remember the convenience of starter kits – package everything your customer will need to begin a new activity – painting, camping, running, etc. – in a bundle for simple buying decisions.

Package your upsell: This can also be called a chain of purchasing. It includes the products or services your client will need to use your product or service. Won't they need leather protector for their new boots? If they've run out of oil paints, how's their supply of brushes, acrylics or canvases? By packaging these clearly related products together, you are making their shopping experience faster and more convenient.

Offer a Customer Loyalty Program:

There are a number of ways to structure your rewards and loyalty program, depending on the type of business and level of technological resources available to you. Customer loyalty programs have a huge advantage – they help build your database of customer information and in most cases allow you to view and analyze purchasing patterns. Here are the most popular:

Every 6th (or 10th) Visit on Us: This works well for business that rely on repeat visits from their customers – like hair salons, coffee shops, auto maintenance, etc. Customers receive a card with store information on the front, and space for stamps or initials on the back. Remember that while 10 is a nice even number, it may be too far in the future for some customers (especially for services that are three to six weeks apart). The idea of six visits is more manageable.

Reward Dollars: This is the Canadian Tire model. For every dollar your customer spends in store, they receive a small portion back in store credit (i.e., Canadian Tire money). The store credit is in the form of printed dollars, branded with your company logo and contact information, and serves as a reminder each time a client opens their wallet.

Reward Points: Another common value-add strategy is a rewards points system. Most grocery stores use this incentive, as well as credit card companies. This works the same as rewards dollars, where a certain number of points are accumulated based on each dollar spent in store. Points can then be spent in store, or on products you have brought in for "rewards points holders" only. This strategy also allows you to feature products with "extra point's value" instead of discounting prices.

Membership Amenities: Instead of points or dollars, you can offer VIP treatment for members, when they sign up for or purchase a membership. This may include occasional discounts, but is primarily centered around perks like "while you wait" amenities, skipping the line, free delivery, etc. You can also produce membership cards.

The sky is the limit when it comes to ways that you can provide added value. Be original and unique in whatever you choose to do and be honest in the presentation. Remember, the customer may not remember your name or your product but the will remember how you made them "feel" and that is critical.

5. Creating a Powerful Offer

"I'm not going to beat around this bush on this one: Your offer is the granite foundation of your marketing campaign."

Get it right, and everything else will fall into place. Your headline will grab readers, your copy will sing, your ad layout will hardly matter, and you will have customers running to your door.

Get it wrong, and even the best looking, best-written campaign will sink like the Titanic.

A powerful offer is an irresistible offer. It's an offer that gets your audience excited and clamoring over each other all the way to your door. An offer that makes your readers pick up the phone and open their wallets.

Irresistible offers make your potential customers think, "I'd be crazy not to take him up on that," or "An offer like this doesn't come around very often." They instill a sense of emotion, of desire, and ultimately, urgency. They should convey a feeling of quality and timeliness so make sure these are built into the offer.

Make it easy for customers to purchase from you the first time, and spend your time keeping them coming back.

I'll say it again: **get it right, and everything else will fall into place.**

The Crux of Your Marketing Campaign

As you work your way through this program, you will find that nearly every chapter discusses the importance of a powerful offer as related to your marketing strategy or promotional campaign.

There's a reason for this. The powerful offer is often the primary reason a customer will open their wallets. It is how you generate leads, and then convert them into loyal customers. The more dramatic, unbelievable, and valuable the offer is the more dramatic and unbelievable the response will be.

Many companies spend thousands of dollars on impressive marketing campaigns in glossy magazines and big city newspapers. They send massive direct mail campaigns on a regular basis; yet don't receive an impressive or massive response rate.

These companies do not yet understand that simply providing information on their company and the benefits of their product is not enough to get customers to act. There is no reason to pick up the phone or visit the store, *right now*.

Your powerful, irresistible offer can:

- Increase leads

- Drive traffic to your website or business

- Move old product

- Convert leads into customers

- Build your customer database

What Makes a Powerful Offer?

A powerful offer is one that makes the most people respond, and take action. It gets people running to spend money on your product or service.

Powerful offers nearly always have an element of *urgency*

and of *scarcity*. They give your audience a reason to act immediately, instead of put it off until a later date.

Urgency relates to time. The offer is only available until a certain date, during a certain period of the day, or if you act within a few hours of seeing the ad. The customer needs to act now to take advantage of the offer.

Scarcity related to quantity. There are only a certain number of customers who will be able to take advantage of the offer. There may be a limited number of spaces, a limited number of products, or simply a limited number of people the business will provide the offer to. Again, this requires that customer acts immediately to reap the high value for low cost.

Powerful offers also:

Offer great value. Customers perceive the offer as having great value – more than a single product on its own, or the product at its regular price. It is clear that the offer takes the reader's needs and wants into consideration.

Make sense to the reader. They are simple and easy to understand if read quickly. Avoid percentages – use half off or 2 for 1 instead of 50% off. There are no "catches" or requirements; no fine print.

Seem logical. The offer doesn't come out of thin air. There is a logical reason behind it – a holiday, end of season, anniversary celebration, or new product. People can get suspicious of offers that seem "too good to be true" and have no apparent purpose.

Provide a premium. The offer provides something extra to the customer, like a free gift, or free product or service. They feel they are getting something extra for no extra cost. Premiums are perceived to have more value than discounts.

Remember that when your target market reads your offer, they will be asking the following questions:

1. What are you offering me?

2. What's in it for me?

3. What makes me sure I can believe and trust you?

4. How much do I have to pay for it?

The Most Powerful Types of Offers

Decide what kind of offer will most effectively achieve your objectives.   Are you trying to generate leads, convert customers, build a database, move old product off the shelves, or increase sales? Consider what type of offer will be of most value to your ideal customers – what offer will make them act quickly.

Free Offer

This type of offer asks customers to act immediately in exchange for something free. This is a good strategy to use to build a customer database or mailing list. Offer a free consultation, free consumer report, or other item of low cost to you but of high perceived value.

You can also advertise the value of the item you are offering for free. For example, act now and you'll receive a free consultation, worth $75 dollars. This will dramatically increase your lead generation, and allow you to focus on conversion when the customer responds.

The Value Added Offer

Add additional services or products that cost you very little, and combine them with other items to increase their attractiveness. This increases the perception of value in the customer's mind, which will justify increasing the price of a product or service without incurring extra hard costs to your business.

Package, Bundle or Kit Offer

Package your products or services together in a logical way to increase the perceived value as a whole. Discount the value of the package by a small margin, and position it as a "start-up kit" or "special package." By packaging goods of mixed values, you will be able to close more high-value sales. For example: including a free desk-jet printer with every computer purchase.

Premium Offer

Offer a bonus product or service with the purchase of another. This strategy will serve your bottom line much better than discounting. This includes 2 for 1 offers, offers that include free gifts and in-store credit with purchases over a specific dollar amount.

Urgency Offer

As I mentioned above, offers that include an element of urgency enjoy a better response rate, as there is a reason for your customers to act immediately. Give the offer a deadline or limit the number of spots available.

Guarantee Offer

Offer to take the risk of making a purchase away from your customers. Guarantee the performance or results of your product or service, and offer to compensate the customer with their money back if they are not satisfied. This will help overcome any fear or reservations about your product, and make it more likely for your leads to become customers.

How You Can Develop Your Powerful Offer

1. Pick a single product or service.

Focus on only one product or service – or one product or service *type* – at a time. This will keep your offer clear, simple, and easy to understand. This can be an area of your business you wish to grow, or old product that you need to move off the shelves.

2. Decide what you want your customers to do.

What are you looking to achieve from your offer? If it is to generate more leads, then you'll need your customer to contact you. If it is to quickly sell old product, you'll need your customer to come into the store and buy it. Do you want them to visit your website? Sign up for your newsletter? How long do they have to act? Be clear about your call to action, and state it clearly in your offer.

3. Dream up the biggest, best offer.

First, think of the biggest, best things you could offer your customers – regardless of cost and ability. Don't limit yourself to a single type of offer, combine several types of offers to increase value. Offer a premium, plus a guarantee, with a package offer. Then take a look at what you've created, and make the necessary changes so it is realistic.

4. Run the numbers.

Finally, make sure the offer will leave you with some profit – or at least allow you to break even. You don't want to publish an outrageous offer that will generate a tremendous number of leads, but leave you broke. Remember that each customer has an acquisition cost, as well as a lifetime value. The amount of their first purchase may allow you to break even, but the amount of their subsequent purchases may make you a lovely profit.

5. Test then; deliver your final version consistently.

6. Monitor and rework your offer or replace it with a new one.

6. Searching for Immediate Sales

"If you're a business owner, you're also a salesperson."

You've had to sell the bank to get them to loan you your start-up capital. You've had to sell the best employees on why they should work for your business. You've had to convince your business partner, spouse, and friends why your business idea is a good one.

Now you have to repeatedly sell your product or service to your customers.

The ability to sell effectively and efficiently is one every successful business owner has cultivated, and continues to develop. It can be a complicated and time consuming task; one that you will have to continually work on throughout your career in order to be – and stay – successful.

Fortunately, making sales is a step-by-step process that can be learned, customized, and continuously improved. There are a wide range of tools available to help and support your sales efforts.

You don't have to be the most outgoing, enthusiastic person to be successful at sales. You don't even have to be a good public speaker. All you need is an understanding of the basic sales process, and a genuine passion for what you are selling.

Sales 101

As I said before, making sales is a process. There are clear, step-by-step actions that can be taken and result in a sale.

The sales process varies according to the type of business, type of customers and type of product or service that is offered; however, the core steps are the same. Similarly, sales training varies from individual to individual, but the core skills and abilities remain the same.

Here is a basic seven-step process that you can follow, or fine tune to suit your unique products and services. Remember that each step is important, and builds on the step previous. It is essential to become adept at each step, instead of solely focusing on closing the sale.

1. Preparation

Make sure you have prepared for your meeting, presentation, or day on the sales floor. You have complete control of this part of the sales process, so it is important to do everything you can to set the stage for your success.

- Understand your product or service inside and out.
- Prepare all the necessary materials, and organize them neatly.
- Keep your place of business tidy and organized. Reface product on shelves.
- Ensure you appear professional and well groomed.
- Do some research on your potential client and brainstorm to find common ground.

2. Build a Relationship

The first few minutes you spend with a potential customer set the stage for the rest of your interaction. First impressions are everything. According to research you have roughly 30 seconds to impress the potential client enough to continue the conversation. Your goal in the second step is to relax the customer and begin to develop a relationship with them. Establishing a real relationship with your customer will create trust.

- Make a great first impression: shake hands, make eye contact, and introduce yourself.
- Remain confident and professional, but also personable.
- Mirror their speech and behavior.
- Begin with general questions and small talk.
- Show interest in them and their place of business.
- Notice and comment on positives.
- Find some common ground on which to relate.

3. Discuss Needs + Wants

Once you have spent a few moments getting to know your prospect, start asking open-ended questions to discover some of their needs and wants. If they have come to you on the sales floor, ask what brought them in the store. If you are meeting them to present your product or service, ask why they are interested in, or what criteria they have in mind for that product or service.

- If you are making a sales presentation, ask for a few moments at the outset to outline the purpose of your visit, as well as how you have structured the presentation.
- Listen intently, and repeat back information you are not sure you understand.
- Ask open-ended questions to get them talking. The longer they talk, the more insight they are providing you into their needs and purchase motivations.
- Ask clarifying questions about their responses.
- If you become sure the customer is going to buy your product or service, begin to ask questions

specific to the offering. i.e., what size/color do you prefer?

4. Present the Solution

Once you have a solid understanding of what they are looking for, or what issue they are looking to resolve, you can begin to present the solution: your product or service.

- Explain how your product or service will solve their problem or meeting their needs. If several products apply, begin by presenting the mid-level product.
- Illustrate your points with anecdotes about other happy customers, or awards the product or service has earned.
- Use hypothetical examples featuring your customer. Encourage them to picture a scenario after their purchase.
- Begin by describing the benefits of the product, then follow up with features and advantages.
- Watch your customer's behavior as you speak, and ask further qualifying questions in response to body language and verbal comments.
- Give the customer an opportunity to ask you questions or provide feedback about each product or service after you have described or explained it.
- Ask closed-ended questions to gain agreement.

5. Overcome Objections

As you present the product or service, take note of potential objections by asking open-ended questions and monitoring body language. Expect that objections will arise and prepare for it. Consider brainstorming a list of all potential objections, and writing down your responses.

- Repeat the objection back to the customer to ensure you understand them correctly.
- Empathize with what they have said, and then provide a response that overcomes the objection.
- Confirm that the answer you have provided has overcome their objection by repeating yourself.

The Eight Most Common Objections
1. The product or service does not seem valuable to me.
2. There is no reason for me to act know. I will wait.
3. It's safest not to make a decision right away.
4. There is not enough money for the purchase.
5. The competitor or another department offers a better product.
6. There are internal issues between people or departments.
7. The relationship with the decision maker is strained.
8. There is an existing contract in place with another business.

6. Close

This is an important part of the sales process that should be handled delicately. Deciding when to close is a judgment call that must be made in the moment during the sale. Ideally, you have presented a solution to their problem, overcome objections, and have the customer in a place where they are ready to buy.

Here are some questions to ask before you close the sale:

- Does my prospect agree that there is value in my product or service?
- Does my prospect understand the features and benefits of the product or service?
- Are there any remaining objections that must be handled?
- What other factors could influence my prospect's decision to buy?
- Have I minimized the risk involved in the purchase, and provided some level of urgency?

Once you have determined it is time to make the sale, here are some sample statements you can use to get the process rolling:

- So, should we get started?
- Shall I grab a new one from the back?
- If you just give me your credit card, I can take care of the transaction while you continue browsing.
- When would you like the product delivered?
- We can begin next month if we receive payment by the end of the week.
- Can I email you a draft contract tomorrow?

7. Service + Follow-up

Once you have made the sale, your work is not over. You want to ensure that that customer will become a loyal, repeat customer, and that they will refer their friends to your business.

Ask them to be in your customer database, and keep in touch with regular newsletters. Follow up with a phone call or drop by to ask how they are enjoying the product or service, and if they have any further questions or needs you can assist them with.

I find that an **"Attitude of Gratitude"**, is critical to maintaining your customers over the long run. I suggest you follow-up at 6 months, 1 year or more post sale, depending on the frequency of purchase and customer life span of your product or service. The focus of this should be personal not business related.

This contact opportunity will also allow you ask for a referral, or an up sell. At the very least, it will ensure you are continuing to foster and build a relationship with the client.

Up selling

Up selling is simply inviting your customers to spend more money in your business by purchasing additional products or services. This could include more of the same product, complementary products, or impulse items.

Regardless, up selling is an effective way to increase profits and create loyal clients – without spending any money to acquire the business. These clients are already purchasing from you – which means they perceive value in what you have to offer – so take the information you have gained in the sales process and offer them a little bit more.

You experience up selling on a daily basis. From "do you want fries with that?" to "have you heard about our product protection program?" companies across the globe have tapped into and trained their staff on the value of the up sell.

Up selling is truly rooted in good customer service. If your client purchases a new computer printer, you'll need to make sure they have the cords required to connect it to the computer, regular and photo paper, and color and black and white ink.

If you don't suggest these items, they may arrive home and realize they do not have all the materials needed to use the product. They may choose to purchase those materials somewhere closer, cheaper, or more helpful.

Customer education is another form of up selling. What if you customer doesn't realize that you sell a variety of printer paper and stationery in addition to computer hardware like printers? Take every opportunity to educate your customer on the products and services you offer that may be of interest to them.

An effective way of implementing an up sell system into your business is simply by creating add-on checklists for the products or services you offer. Each item has a list of related items that your customer may need. This will encourage your staff to develop the habit of asking for the up sell.

Other up sell strategies can be implemented:

- **At the point of sale**. This is a great place for impulse items like candy, flashlights, nail scissors, etc.
- **In a newsletter**. This is an effective strategy for customer education.
- **In your merchandising**. Place strips of impulse items near related items. For example, paper clips with paper and pens near binders.
- **Over the phone**. If someone is placing an order for delivery, offer additional items in the same shipment for convenience.

- **With new products**. Feature each new product or service that you offer prominently in your business, and ask your staff to mention it to every customer.

Sales Team

Employing a team of strong salespeople

What Makes a Good Salesperson?

There are a lot of salespeople out there – but what qualities and skills make a great salesperson? These are the attributes you will want to find or develop in your team:

- Willingness to continuously learn and improve sales skills
- Sincerity in relating to customers and providing solutions to their objectives
- An understanding of the company's big picture
- A communication style that is direct, polite, and professional
- Honesty and respect for other team members, customers, as well as the competition.
- Ability to manage time
- Enthusiastic
- Inquisitive
- A great listener
- Ability to quickly interpret, analyze, and respond to information during the sales process
- Ability to connect and develop relationships of trust with potential clients
- Professional appearance

Team Building – Keeping Your Team Together

In many businesses, sales is a department or a whole team of people who work together to generate leads and convert customers. Effective management of your sales team is a skill every business owner should cultivate.

Team building, recruitment, and training will be discussed in later sections, but take some time to consider the following aspects of managing a sales team:

Communication

- Are targets and results regularly reviewed?
- Are opportunities for input regularly provided?
- Do sales staff members have a clear understanding of what is expected?
- Do all staff members know daily, weekly, and quarterly targets?

Performance Management – Formal & Informal

- Are sales staff members motivated to reach targets or wishful thinking?
- Are sales staff recognized and rewarded once those targets are reached?
- Are there opportunities for skills training and development?
- Do staff members have broad and comprehensive product or industry knowledge?
- Is there opportunity for growth within the company?
- Is performance regularly reviewed?

Operations

- Do you have a solid understanding of your sales numbers (revenue, profit, margins)?
- Are your sales processes regularly reviewed?
- Do you have a variety of sales scripts prepared?
- Do you measure conversion rates?
- How are your leads generated?

Sales Tools are Great If Used

Every salesperson should have an arsenal of tools on hand to assist them in the sales process. These tools can act as aids while a sale is taking place, or help to foster continual learning and development of the salesperson's skills and approach.

The list below includes some popular sales tools. Add to this list with other resources that are specific to your business or industry.

Tool	Description + Benefit
Scripts	Used for incoming and outgoing telemarketing, cold calls, door-to-door sales, in-store sales Create several different scripts throughout your business Maintains consistency in your sales approach Revise and renew your scripts regularly

Presentation Materials	High-quality information about your product or service Forms: PowerPoint presentation, brochure, product sheets, proposal Serves as an outline of your sales presentation, and keeps you on task
Colleagues	A source of help and advice, especially when you are on the same team or sell similar products Also a source of support
Customer Databases	An accurate, up-to-date database of customer contact information and contact history Used to stay in touch with clients Can also be used for direct mail and follow-up telemarketing
The Internet	A powerful resource for sales help and advice Information to help improve your sales process Online sales coaching Source for product knowledge
Ongoing Training	Constant improvement of your sales skills Constant increase in product knowledge Investment in yourself and your company

8 Tips for Better Sales

- **Dress for the sale.** Dress professionally, appear well put together and maintain good hygiene. Ensure you are not only dressed professionally, but *appropriately.* Would your client feel more comfortable if you wore a suit, or jeans and blazer?
- **Speak their language.** Show you understand their industry or culture, and use phrases your customer understands. This may require researching industry jargon or common phrases. Remember to avoid using words and phrases that are used in the sales process: sold, contract, telemarketing, finance, interest, etc. Doing so will help break down the salesperson/customer barrier.
- **Ooze positivity**. Show up or answer the phone with a smile, and leave your personal or business issues behind. Be enthusiastic about what you have to offer, and how that offering will benefit your customer. Reflect this not only in your voice, but also in your body language.
- **Deliver a strong pitch or presentation**. Be confident and convincing. Leave self-doubt at the door, and walk in assuming the sale. Take time to explain complex concepts, and always connect what you're saying to your audience in a specific way.
- **Be a poster-child for good manners**. Accept any amenity you're offered, listen intently, don't interrupt, don't show up late, have a strong handshake, and give everyone you are speaking to equal attention.
- **Avoid sensitive subjects**. Politics, religion, swearing, sexual innuendos and racial comments are absolutely off-limits. So are negative comments about other customers or the competition.

- **Create a real relationship.** Icebreakers and small talk are not just to pass the time before your presentation. They are how relationships get established. Show genuine interest in everything your customer has to say. Ask questions about topics you know they are passionate. Speak person to person, not salesperson to customer. Remember everything.

- **Know more than you need to.** Impress clients with comprehensive knowledge – not only of your product or service – but also of the people who use that product or service, and industry trends. Been seen as an expert in order to build trust and respect.

7. Have Clients that Pay, Stay & Refer!

"Successful businesses that see sustained growth have a double-edged marketing strategy. They focus their marketing efforts outward – on new potential customers – as well as inward – on existing customers and referral business."

When it comes to marketing and generating more income, most business owners are focused outward.

They've carefully established and segmented their target market, and created specific offers and messages for each market segment. They spend thousands of dollars in advertising and direct mail campaigns in hot pursuit of more leads, more customers, and more foot traffic.

While this is an effective way to build a business, it is costly and time consuming. It requires constant and consistent effort, and while this approach does generate results, those results quickly disappear when the effort stops or becomes less intense.

These successful businesses have leveraged their existing efforts to generate more revenue. Simply put, their customers buy from them over and over again.

For most businesses, this is the easiest way to increase their revenues. Simple customer loyalty strategies and outstanding customer service are often all you need to dramatically increase your sales – from the customers you already have.

The Cost of Your Customers

Do you know how much it costs your business to buy new customers?

Each new customer that walks through your door or visits your website — with the exception of referrals — has cost you money to acquire. You have spent money on advertising and promotions to generate leads and turn those leads into customers.

For example, if you have placed an ad in your local newspaper for $1,000, and the ad brings in 10 customers, you have paid $100 to acquire each customer. You would need to ensure each of those customers spent at least $200 to cover your margin and break even.

Alternately, if you spent two hours of your time and $10 per month on an email marketing program to send a newsletter to your existing database of customers, and you bring in 10 customers as a result — each customer has cost you $1.

Generating more repeat business means focusing on the marketing strategies that aim to keep your existing customers instead of purchase new ones — effectively reducing the cost of attracting new customers to your business.

These strategies are simple to implement, and don't require much time investment. Just a solid understanding of how to make customers want to come back and spend more of their money

Keeping Your Customers

Marketing strategies that focus on keeping your current customer base are easy and enjoyable to implement. They allow you to build real relationships with the people you do business with, instead of dealing with a revolving door of people on the other end of your sales process.

Repeat customers create a community of people around your business that presumably share the same needs, desires and frustrations. The information you gain from these customers (no-cost market research) can help you strengthen your understanding of your target audience, and more accurately segment it.

Remember – generally, 80% of your revenue comes from 20% of your customers. Always focus on these customers. They are ideal customers that you want to recruit, and hold on to. Another factor is that up to 68% of your customers may leave because of perceived indifference so staying focused is critical.

Customer Service: Make them love buying from you

Every business – even those with excellent service standards can improve the service they provide their customers. Customer service seems to be a dying concept in most businesses; more focus seems to be placed on the speed of the transaction. These days you can even go to the grocery store now and not speak to a single sales associate thanks to self-serve checkouts.

To improve your company's customer service standards, take a survey of your customers and your employees to brainstorm ways you can improve the experience of buying from your business. Listen and then act to improve!

Successful customer service standards – those that make your customers buy – are:

Consistent. The standards are the responsibility of every person in your organization. Expectations are clear and followed through. Customers know what to expect, and choose your business because of those expectations.

Convenient. It is nearly effortless for the customer to spend money at your place of business. Convenience can take many forms – location, product selection, value-added services like delivery – and it is also consistent.

Customer-driven. The service the customer receives is exactly how they would like to be treated when buying your product or service. It is reflective of your target market, and appropriate to their lifestyle. Customers would probably not appreciate white linen tablecloths at a fast food restaurant, but they would appreciate a 2-minutes or less guarantee.

Newsletters: Keep in touch with your customers

A regular newsletter is an easy, time-effective, and inexpensive marketing strategy to implement. Unfortunately, many small businesses think these are too time consuming and too expensive to adopt as part of their marketing strategy.

The most popular type of newsletter distribution is email. This will cost your business as little at $10 per month for an email marketing service subscription, and can be customized to your unique branding.

Look at sharing articles with an association in a company like growthpod.com. This is a very simple concept where various firms cooperate with you to promote each other monthly.

Here is an easy five-step process to starting a company newsletter:

> **1. Pick your audience.** New customers? Market segment? Existing customers?

> **2. Choose what you're going to say.** Company news? Feature product? New offer?

> **3. Determine how you're going to say it.** Articles? Bullet points? Pictures?

> **4. Decide how it's going to get to your audience.** Email? Mail? In-store? Search out tools available!

> **5. Track your results.** How many people opened it? Read it? Took action?

Value Added Service: Give them happy surprises

Adding value to your business is an effective way of getting your customers back. Every person I know would choose a mattress store that offered free delivery over one that did not. It's that simple.

There are many ways to add value to your business, including:

- o **Feature your expertise.** Use your knowledge to provide additional value to your customers. Offer a free consumer guide or report with every purchase.

- o **Add convenience services.** Offer a service that makes their purchase easier, or more convenient. The best example of this is free shipping or delivery.

- o **Package complementary services.** Packaging like items together creates an increase in perceived value. This is great for start-up kits.

○ **Offer new products or services**. Feature top of the line or exclusive products, available only at your business. Offer a new service or profile a new staff member with niche expertise.

Value added services generate repeat customers in one of two ways:

1. Impress them on their first visit. Impress you customer with great service, a product that meets their needs, and then wow them with something extra that they weren't expecting. Get them to associate the experience of dealing with your business with happy surprises, and create a perception of higher value.

2. Entice them to come back. The introduction of a new value-added service can be enough to convince a customer to buy from you again. Their initial purchase established a trust and knowledge of your business and its processes. They will want to "be included" in anything new you have to offer – especially if there is exclusivity. It is easier to attract clients that have purchased from you than potential clients who have not.

Customer Loyalty Programs: Give them incentives.

Another simple way to keep in touch with existing customers and keep them coming back to you is to create a customer loyalty program.

These programs do not have to be complicated or costly, and are relatively easy to maintain once they have been implemented. These programs help you gain more information on your customers and their purchasing habits.

Here are some examples of simple loyalty programs that you can implement:

Free product or service. Give them every 10th (or 6th) product or service free. Produce stamp cards with your logo and contact information on it.

Reward dollars. Give them a certain percentage of their purchase back in money that can only be spent in-store. Produce "funny money" with your logo and brand.

Rewards points. Give them a certain number of points for every dollar they spend. These points can be spent in-store, or on special items you bring in for points only.

Membership amenities. Give members access to VIP amenities that are not available to other customers. Produce member cards or give out member numbers.

Remember that in order for this strategy to work, you and your team have to understand, promote and live it. The program in itself becomes a product that you sell. Your customer must be confident that you care for them and their business.

8. Understand Profit

"As a small business owner, you are in business for one reason: to make money."

Of course, there are other reasons you started or purchased your company. You may love the product you sell, or service you provide. You may love the challenge of turning a floundering company into an overnight success. You may just love being your own boss.

Naturally, this all means nothing if you are not generating enough income to support yourself and your family, as well as the people who work for you.

Nearly all businesses make money. Unless not a single product or service is sold, there is always money coming in. But there is also always money going out. Supplies, wages, marketing, acquisitions and operations all contribute to the expense of just staying in business.

Simply put, profit is the difference between money in and money out. This is the dollar value of your sales, minus the cost of those sales.

In business, you will find that everyone wants to make more money. They want to increase their sales, get more money coming in. **What often gets overlooked is that the true secret to making more money is not increasing sales, but increasing profit.**

What is Profit?

Before you can take steps to increase the profitability of your business, you have to have a solid understanding of:

- types of profit
- what factors influence profit
- what your profit is *right now*

Types of Profit

There are two main types of profit:

Gross Profit

Gross profit is the simplest form of calculating profit. It is simply the money that comes through the cash register, minus the cost of acquiring or providing the products or services.

The formula is:

Total revenue (sales) – cost of goods or services sold = Gross Profit

Net Profit

Net profit is a more accurate reflection of your income. It is calculated by taking your gross profit minus expenses over a specific time period (usually by quarter).

The formula is:

Gross profit – expenses (cost of running a business) = Net Profit

Factors that Influence Profit

Profit is your bottom line. It is the number that falls out the bottom when all other costs and expenses have been taken into consideration. Do you know what contributes to the amount of profit your business ends up with?

There are three main factors that influence profit:

Sales – Your Conversion Rate

The first, and most obvious, factor is the money that comes in the door through sales. In theory, the more sales you make, the more money you bring in, the greater your profits.

The ratio of potential customers to sales is called your conversion rate. This is the percentage of customers you have converted from leads to sales. So, a high conversion rate means more sales, and more money coming in the door.

In addition to your conversion rate is the lifetime value of your clients. It costs much less to convince a customer to make repeat purchases than it does to acquire new clients.

Costs – Your Product/Service Margins

The second factor is the cost of your offering – what your product or service costs you to acquire or provide. If you sell a product, this is the wholesale price you pay for the product. If you offer a service, it is the cost of your (or your employee's) time plus any materials used.

Your margin is the difference between the price you pay and the price your customers pay. If you buy toothpaste for $1 from the wholesaler, and you sell it for $3, your margin is $2. If a haircut costs $20 in materials and service, and the customer pays $50, your margin is $30.

Expenses – The Cost of Doing Business

The final factor is the cost of running your business – those not directly related to the specific product or service you offer. Expenses include:

- Office or store lease

- Computer equipment lease

- Employee salaries

- Utilities

- Marketing + advertising

Do You Know What Your Profit Is?

It only makes sense that you need to know where you are to determine how to get to where you want to be. This applies to any plan to create in business.

Before you can increase your profits, you need to have an understanding of where your profits are currently – and if you're making any at all. The next section will take you through a process to review the specific factors that affect your business's profitability, and ultimately determine how much profit you are currently bringing in.

Taking Stock of Your Profits

Before you devise a strategy to increase your profits, you need to take a good long look at the money your business brings in, and the money you spend to run your business. You may wish to sit down with your accountant or bookkeeper to analyze the financial information that is available to you.

Decide on a specific time period to review – one that makes sense to your business, and one that will give you the most realistic picture of your business performance.

This will depend if your operation is cyclical, or remains steady throughout the year. Usually, the previous quarter or the previous four quarters will give you enough of an indication.

Here is a general of items to review:

- Total revenue
- Total cost of goods or services
- Total cost of operations (overhead), including:
    - Employee wages
    - Recruitment
    - Business development
    - Utilities
    - Rent or mortgage
    - Office supplies
    - Computer leases
    - Incidentals
    - Total cost of marketing campaigns

Total profit after costs and expenses for this time period:

_____.

The Five Factors that Eat Your Profits

It is easy for business owners to compare their organizations to the apparent success of their competitors. Joe's Pizza may always be teaming with customers and appear to be making money hand over fist, while your pizza shop may have slower, but more steady business.

It is important to remember that a business with extraordinary sales figures is not necessarily a profitable one. Sales are just one element of your profit calculation.

Here are some other elements to think about when reviewing the profitability of your business:

1. Impulse Spending

How often do you make purchases for your business operations? I'm not talking about acquiring new goods and services, but upgrading computers, taking your team out for lunch, or leasing a new color photocopier.

Do you allow your staff to make purchases on your behalf? Who reviews these decisions? Take a look not only at *what* you buy, but *how* spending is structured in your company.

2. Small Margins

As we discussed in the previous section, your margins are the difference between your cost and the customer's cost to purchase your goods or services.

Typically, businesses that offer a variety of products will have both products with large margins, and products with small margins. The products with large margins generate the most income, so these are the products that staff should be focused on selling.

What many businesses overlook is that products with small margins will never generate a high level of income, no matter how many you sell. A store stocked with small margin items will never be able to increase their profit because they have so little margin to work with, unless they can manage inventory turn.

3. Your Customers

This may seem like a backwards way of thinking. Your customers spend money, so they are a positive factor in your profit calculation, right?

This is true for most of your customers. But remember the 80/20 rule of business – 80% of your revenue comes from

20% of your customers. These are your top 20%, or ideal customers. What about your bottom 20%? The group of clients who ask for the moon and never stop complaining.

These clients can be a huge drain on both your staff resources and your financial resources. Their true value to your business is minimal – they cost more than they bring in. Fire them!

4. Loan Interest

How many business loans do you currently have? Credit card debit? Overdraft? The interest you pay on these loans can be a substantial monthly cost to your business.

A loan from a bank is just like any other product. You can shop around for the best deal. Consider consolidating or restructuring your debit to minimize interest payments. Plan to search around for the best rate on a regular basis – every few months or quarter.

5. Vendors

Do you purchase your goods and services from a wholesaler or retailer? How long have you been in business with this company? What do you pay for goods and services relative to your competitors? Be cognizant of quality issues based on prices offered. Cheaper is not always better, look deep to ensure it is the quality your company provides on a consistent basis.

Ensure that you are dealing with as direct a vendor as possible to minimize your acquisition costs and increase your margins. If you have been doing business with a particular vendor for an extended period of time, consider renegotiating your business arrangement.

The Basics of Increasing Profit

Your Profitability Goal

Now that you have an understanding of the current profitability of your company, it is time to look at ways to increase your bottom line.

Like all other aspects of your business development, you need to have a clear idea of your intention or purpose before you begin any activity. Assuming you wish to increase the profitability of your business, you need to determine by how much and within what time frame.

Create a profit-related goal for your business, and write it here:

_____

_____

Three Ways to Increase Profit

There are countless strategies for increasing profit, but ultimately you can only increase profit in one of three ways:

1. Get More Customers

Use marketing outreach strategies to generate more leads, and convert those leads into more customers. Introduce a new offer, expand your target audience, or approach a new target audience.

2. Get Your Customers to Buy More Often

Use customer loyalty and retention strategies to get your existing customers to buy from you more often. Make it easy for them to come back and do business with you.

You can do this by adding value to your product or service, keeping in touch on a regular basis, and giving your customers incentive to make repeat purchases. Customer service is also an overlooked component of building a repeat client base.

3. Increase Quantity Your Customers Buy

You'll naturally increase your sales when you increase the number of customers and how often they purchase. The final way you can impact your profit is by increasing the average dollar value of each sale.

This can be achieved by up-selling every customer, creating package offers, and finding ways to increase the perceived value of your offering to justify increasing the price.

Managing Costs

One important way to impact the profitability of your business is through cost or spending management. Controlling how much money goes out will help you ensure that a more money stays in your bank account.

Remember, however, that cutting costs can only help increase your profits so much. There is a point where you will no longer be able to reduce expenses, and you will have to focus on increasing sales. Don't sacrifice quality to cut costs.

Why Cut Costs?

Cost cutting may seem like an obvious way of maintaining a healthy business. Overspending is a huge problem for most businesses – and they don't even realize it and it is also one of the primary reasons 80% of small businesses fail.

Reducing costs is a great short-term strategy to boost profits. However, there is a limited amount of impact cost cutting can have on the bottom line, so it is an ineffective long term strategy.

Initially cost management can help you to generate more capital. A business that closely monitors and controls its spending is a much more desirable loan candidate than a business that spends freely.

Most importantly, this strategy, if balanced correctly, will help keep your business profitable through high and low periods. It's easy to spend money when your company is doing well, but this leaves little in the "just in case" account for downturns in the economy or unexpected expenses. Be creative in cost cutting

Where Can I Cut Costs?

Financing

As I mentioned, interest rates are a big culprit when it comes to eating profits. Take stock of how much money you are spending on a monthly basis in loan and interest payments. Can this be reduced? Is there another bank that will offer you a lower rate? Is there a way to consolidate these loans into a single, low-interest account?

Alternatively, if your business is doing well and has a large amount of money sitting in the bank; consider investing it or placing it in a high-interest savings account. Let your money make you money instead of spending it on unnecessary business luxuries.

Suppliers or Vendors

Again, as mentioned above, make sure the price you pay for goods and services – for resale or internal use – is the lowest you can find.   Try to deal directly with the manufacturer or distributor, and renegotiate discounts and contracts with your vendors every year. Always keep an eye on quality when discussing this topic with vendors.

Hours of Operation

Evaluate the hours you are open for business each day, and why you have chosen the specific timeframe.   Is it to compete with the competitors? Is it because you can serve the highest number of customers? Each hour you are open for business costs you money, so make sure you are operating under the most ideal timeframe.

Staffing, Wages, and Compensation

This can be a sensitive subject for any business owner or employee. It is important to look at staffing redundancies and capacity levels – as well as hiring needs – when evaluating cost management strategies.

Do you need to hire new staff, or can you build capacity within your existing employees? Is there another way to compensate staff, or provide performance incentives that are non-monetary, have a high perceived value, and inexpensive for your business? Remember to take time and care when implementing any changes in this area of cost management. Know the value that each person brings to the business and how effectively they are filling the role.

Place of Business

If you operate an office in a downtown metropolis, you are going to have substantially higher operating costs than a competitor who runs an office just outside the city limits.

Make sure you can justify your location, and the amount of money you spend to be there. Consider the following questions:

- Are my customers impacted by where I do business?
- Do my customers need to visit my office?
- How easily can they access my office? Is there an easy ingress and egress from the parking?
- What impression does my business need to present?
- Do I need parking facilities?
- Do I need to be visible?
- Do I have staff to employ?
- Am I near public transit, lunch outlets, and other amenities?
- Do I need access after business hours?
- Should I lease or buy?
- What other costs are specific to this location?

Eliminate the invisible!

What could you and your staff live without? What wouldn't you notice if it just disappeared one day? Take stock of expenses that are not being properly used or appreciated. Think of amenity-based items, or convenience costs, like:

- Gym Memberships
- Morning refreshments (muffins, donuts, etc.)
- Publication Subscriptions

- Designer coffee and tea
- Fancy collateral packaging

Your Pricing Strategy

The cost of your goods and services have a direct impact on the money you bring in. Your pricing strategy is so important to your business that can even determine your success.

Deciding how much to charge for your product or service is a challenging task. You need to factor in your own costs, the product or service's perceived value, and the going rate. Ultimately, you want to be able to charge as much as possible for each item, without overpricing yourself out business.

Avoid the Lowest Pricing Strategy

The days of the lowest price guarantee and pricing wars are over – especially for small businesses. The "big players" in the marketplace will quickly put you out of business if you try to compete on price. Their pockets are deeper and they have lower operating costs due to their sheer size. They can afford to – you can't.

Clearly Position Your Company and Your Offering

How do you want your target market to view your business, and your products? Are you trying to create an image of high quality? High value? Reliable service? Make sure your pricing is consistent with the image you are trying to project. If you are operating a high end spa – you're not competing with the budget nail salon down the street, so your prices should be considerably higher.

Have a Good Working Knowledge of Your Margins

Know how much the product or service costs you to offer before you establish a price. Do these costs remain consistent, or do they fluctuate? Restaurants that offer high quality meat and seafood often price their meals at "market rates" as opposed to fixed rates. Calculate the fixed and variable costs associated with your product or service. You will want to work the cost of the product or service, a percentage of your overhead, and your own profit into the cost of each item.

Pay Attention to Factors Beyond Your Control

Be aware of any government or industry regulations on the price of your product or services. Some laws will actually limit how much you can charge for standard services. For medical and dental services, most insurance companies will put a cap on how much a customer will be compensated for each service.

Price with a Purpose

Your pricing strategy should be purpose focused. What exactly are you trying to do by setting your prices at certain levels? Here are some potential reasons for pricing strategies:

- Short-term profit increase
- Long-term profit increase
- Customer generation
- Product positioning
- Revenue maximization
- Increase margins
- Market differentiation
- Survival

Pricing Strategies

Cost Plus Pricing

This is the most basic pricing strategy. Set your price at a number that includes:

- Cost of goods or services, based on a specific sales volume
- Percentage of expenses
- Profit margin (markup)
- Simple but based on transparency & accuracy.

Target ROI Pricing

Set your price at a rate that will achieve a specific Return on Investment target. If you need to make $20,000 from 1,000 units – or $20 per unit – then set your price at $20 more than cost, plus expenses.

Value Based Pricing

This can be a bit of an arbitrary pricing strategy, but it can also be the most profitable. Set your price based on the value or added benefit it brings to a customer. For example, if your product only costs you $40 to produce, but will save the customer $2,000 per year in energy costs, a price of $150 or $200 would not appear to be unreasonable in the eyes of the customer.

Psychological Pricing

What messages are you trying to send the customer when they're looking at your prices for your products? Do you offer the best deal? The highest value? These are reasons to choose prices that are higher or lower than the competition.

Pricing Guidelines

Price higher than cost. This may seem obvious, but ensure that your pricing not only covers your costs, but potential fluctuations in sales volume and in the marketplace. If you sell half of your order, will you still make a profit?

Include expenses. If you price to cover your costs, will you also be able to cover your expenses and still see a profit? Your margin needs to pay for your expenses, leave you with something to live on, plus some working capital for the company.

Consider the 'fair' price. What do your consumers think is 'fair' for each service or product? This is impacted by your competitor's price, your company's image (high quality or high value, low cost), and the perceived value of your product or service.

Strategies to Increase Profit

Once you have a concrete understanding of where your business stands today in terms of profitability, minimized your operating costs, and restructured your pricing strategy, you can focus on other strategies to increase profit.

There are countless strategies and tactics that will help you to bring in more customers, get those customers to come back, and get those customers to spend more when they do.

Here is a list of ideas, many of which are covered in detail in other sections of this program:

- Advertise
- Establish an online presence
- Sell more high margin items

- Generate more leads
- Focus on referral business
- Increase customer loyalty and repeat business
- Increase conversion rates
- Restructure your team
- Reinvent your product
- Sell your intellectual capital

9. Staff Recruitment Training and Development

"The people you hire to work for your business can be your biggest assets and your biggest headaches."

They can support and help you to achieve the vision you have for your company – but they can also prevent you from reaching that vision.

Too many businesses overlook the role of employee recruitment and retention when planning for the success of their organization. Staffing is an important exercise that needs to be purpose driven and strategic, just like marketing.

It is vital to understand in today's market that the relationship between employee and employer is a two-way street. Now, more than ever, employees have a "what's in it for me?" attitude that extends beyond salary and benefits expectations into soft benefits, incentive and reward programs. The days of simple compensation structures are over.

Now, this may sound like a big headache, but it's actually a good thing! With some simple systems and open dialogue, you will be able to effectively create – and keep – your dream team.

The Power of Your Dream Team

How much of your own personal time has human resources – staff hiring, firing, issues management, etc. – taken this year? No doubt staff recruitment and retention is one of the biggest challenges facing any business owner today.

The truth is, if you spent half as much time on human resources as you do on marketing, I guarantee your sales would increase dramatically.

Customers know the difference between happy employees and disgruntled ones, and it makes a difference when it comes to purchase decisions. Would you rather have your car serviced by a grumpy mechanic who doesn't feel his good work is rewarded, or a pleasant one who just stepped out a weekly team meeting?

A successful business owner has confidence in the people who work for him, because he believes they are the best people for the job. Employees who know their employer believes in their skills and abilities will go over and above to get the job done, to make the sale.

Successful business owners invest time and money in finding and keeping the right people. These are the people who share and support the collective vision for the company.

I'm not talking about a complicated formula, or a magical concoction. I'm talking about some careful thought and a proactive strategy, vision and mission that will make your business shine from the inside out.

Finding Your Dream Employees

Building a dream team starts by finding and hiring the right people for the job. Sounds simple enough. You post an ad, find someone who has the necessary qualifications, and hire them on.

Not so fast. Recruitment is complex process that can dramatically impact your business operations. Just like finding and securing the right customers, finding and hiring the right candidates requires pro-active planning and careful evaluation.

If you currently work with a recruiting agency to build to your team, now may be a good time to stop and evaluate the effectiveness of their service. While a recruiting agency can save you the time and hassle of working through the hiring process, it can also cost more money in the long run.

I always recommend creating an internal recruitment system, not because recruiting agencies do a bad job, but because no one knows your business like you do.

An internal recruitment system ensures that the true essence of your business culture is communicated – from advertisement to interview. You also have the opportunity to communicate expectations from the outset, instead of relying on the recruiter to relay this information. The middle-man's thoughts and impressions are eliminated, leaving you to make decisions based on your impression of the candidate and no one else's.

Step One: Advertise the Opportunity

The first step in recruiting candidates is obviously letting potential candidates know about the opportunity with your company.

But before you pick up the phone to place a classified ad or post the position online, remember that searching for potential employees requires just as much consideration and planning as general marketing for your business.

You need to ask yourself:

- Who is your ideal candidate?
- What personality type fits best in our culture?
- What are their skills and qualifications?
- What is their personality or demeanor?

- What are they passionate about?
- What are they looking for in a job?
- What unique benefit can I provide for them?

Once you have a mental picture of your candidate, then you can begin to write an ad that will not only reach them, but also inspire them to act (and submit an application).

When writing this ad, be as specific as possible and focus on the benefits of the job. Remember that potential candidates screen job postings with an eye for "what's in it for me." Tell them exactly that.

Here are a couple of sample job postings:

1. Are you the Marketing Assistant we need?

About You:

You're fun, friendly and have a keen eye for detail. You're always two steps ahead of your colleagues, and eager to take on new and exciting challenges.

You'll be the glue that keeps the marketing team operating in a seamless fashion, responsible for website updates, copywriting, event coordination and client relations. You'll be punctual, responsible, and well put together.

You'll ideally have an undergraduate degree in marketing or English, and some previous office experience, but a fast learner with a great attitude will also get our attention.

About Us:

We are a collaborate team of young professionals. We offer a competitive salary, great benefits and performance incentives.

Think you fit the bill? Email your resume and cover letter to John Smith at jsmith@email.com by Friday at 4pm.

2. **Are Computers Your Life?**

About You:

You are smart, outgoing, and a wiz when it comes to computer programming. You're on your friend's speed dial for computer emergencies, large and small. Helping people understand the complex digital world is your passion.

You'll be our Lead Computer Technician, managing our computer repair counter and five Junior Technicians. You'll have great people skills, mounds of patience, and enjoy working as part of a dynamic team.

About Us:

We operate Anytown's leading computer repair store, and are known across the region for our customer service. We work hard, play hard, and offer a competitive benefits package to our employees.

Tell us why this job is for you. Email your resume and cover letter to info@computerworld.com by Thursday, September 23.

Both of these job postings speak directly to a very targeted audience. They're friendly, colloquial, and communicate the job requirements in an informal way.

Every job posting should:

- Be colloquial (written in the way that you talk)
- Be specific, as possible
- Describe benefits
- Include skills, qualifications, duties and job title
- Be written in the present tense
- Have a great headline
- Call the reader to action
- Be simple – in word choice and sentence structure
- Be more exciting than the competition

Now that you have a great ad to post, you need to decide where you are going to publish it. This depends on the level of the job (junior to management) and on the specific type of candidate you are looking to recruit.

Here are the five major places to advertise your opportunity:

Government Employment Center

These are great places to find blue-collar or junior level employees. Candidates register with the center, which keeps their resumes on file. Be cautious with this route – it can produce a wide variety of candidates who are not qualified.

Local Newspaper

This is a great place to post junior to mid-level employment opportunities. You're looking for basic qualifications from local applicants, perhaps even for part-time positions, with minimal cost.

Regional or City Newspaper

Senior employment opportunities that require specific high-level qualifications are best advertised with a broad scope. This incurs a greater cost, but will return a greater variety of candidates.

Online

This is a cheap way to tap into a massive database of job seekers. Post your ad online on sites like, www.indeed.com, www.monster.com or www.workopolis.com and watch the resumes come flooding in. Be prepared to handle the onslaught so you can handle the decision making processes. Too many times I have seen companies fall into analysis paralysis due to the volume of resumes. Many highly qualified job seekers or people who have unique skills and who do not wish to register with a recruitment agency will use these services.

Referrals - Networking

The most ideal way to find candidates is through your existing network – including associates, colleagues, employees, friends and family. These candidates come to you already vetted by a trusted source. You may also wish to consider giving your staff an incentive to refer their qualified friends and associates to you.

You should also brainstorm a list of any other niche areas that your target market may look for a job. Consider industry publications, industry associations, small publications, etc.

Once you've posted your ad, your next step is to manage the inquiries that come flooding in.

Step Two: Screen Candidates

This is one of the most time-consuming aspects of the recruitment process, so you will need to work out a system to manage the response to your job posting.

A system will also allow you ensure you ask all potential candidates the same questions, and provide them with the same information about the role as well as about your company.

> **1. Decide whether all inquiries will be handled by one person or several.** This will depend on your staff resources and capacity. A system will allow multiple employees to assist in the process.
>
> For example, if your candidates have been instructed to submit their resume and cover letter to you through email, designate a single email address and inbox to receiving and responding. This way you or another staff member will not be bombarded by emails, and can designate an hour of time each day to managing the inquiries. If your candidates are calling in, designate a unique phone number or answering machine to this purpose.
>
> **2. Decide how inquiries will be responded to.** This can be as simple as an email acknowledging receipt of the resume, or specific instructions on an answering machine. Ensure everyone receives the same information, and that you receive the same level of information from all candidates (resume, cover letter, portfolio, references, and other relevant information.).
>
> If you have asked candidates to call you instead of submit their resumes through email, create a standard checklist of questions to ask them, as well

as of information to provide them with. You may wish to create a script. Some questions might include:

- What kind of job are you looking for?
- Why do you think you would be well suited to this position?
- Tell me a bit about yourself.
- What makes you interested in our company?

Use this opportunity to get a feel for the applicant's personality, and trust your initial impression. Create a form on which to record this information, and file it with their resume when you receive it.

3. Devise a process for reviewing resumes or applications. The easiest and most time efficient way to do this is in a single session, after the stated deadline, and not as you receive them. You may wish to enlist the assistance of a senior colleague or department employees to provide a second opinion.

Review the resumes and application materials, and divide the applications into three piles: interview, no interview, and maybe. From here you can begin to call candidates and set up a first interview.

It is also a good idea to be in touch with unsuccessful candidates, and politely let them know that you will not be asking them in for an interview. If you anticipate your response rate will be overwhelming, you may wish to consider stating in your advertisement that only successful applicants will be called.

Step Three: First Interview

The first interview is also a screening interview; your objective is to develop a first impression of the candidate as a person, and to determine if they are qualified for the position. If you feel you have found an ideal candidate, this is also your opportunity to convince them to choose your company over any others they may be considering. Good people don't stay in the market long.

Interview Structure

You will need to decide on a structure, or system, for the interview process as well. Will you be conducting the first interviews, or will another manager? Will the interviews be conducted one on one, or will several employees participate? If you are replacing an employee, you may want to consider inviting that employee into the interview to provide insight into the role.

Interview Materials

Just as you are asking the potential candidate to come prepared to the interview, you must be as well.

- Have an outline prepared of what you would like to cover. Topics include: company history, job description, interview questions, compensation structure, availability, and room for advancement.
- Bring two copies of a typed job description. Include all tasks the candidate will be responsible for completing or assisting with.
- A company profile or overview document (other marketing collateral will also work

here).

Interview Attitude

Begin to build a relationship with each applicant. The purpose of the interview is not just to discuss the job description, or for the applicant to get all the interview questions "right." It is to determine if this person has the right attitude for the job, and whether or not they will fit in with the company's culture and its employees.

Keep the interview professional, but make sure the applicant is comfortable. Interviews test our ability to perform under pressure, but you will want to gain an understanding of the applicant's true nature. Remember that even if the applicant is not well suited to the role they have applied for, they may be suited to a future opportunity with the company.

Interview Questions

The questions you decide to ask the candidate are highly specific to your company and the role you are hiring for. Take some time to brainstorm what you really need to know about each person, and what questions you can ask to get that information.

Keep in mind that part of the objective of the first interview is to get a sense of the candidate's personality. You will want to ask questions about their responses, and begin to establish a real relationship with them.

Here are some starter interview questions to get you going:

- Tell me a little bit about your background.
- What has been your first impression of our company/product/services?
- Tell me about a time when...[insert a likely scenario they will encounter in the position]. How did it make you feel? How did you handle the situation?
- What advantages do you feel you have over the other candidates?
- What are your strengths? Weaknesses?
- Tell me about an achievement you're proud of.
- Why did you leave your last position?
- Where do you see yourself in five years?
- ...and so on.

Make sure you take good notes, or ask a junior member of your team to take notes for you. Also record your impression of the candidate after each interview. You will want to be able to reflect on each interview before inviting the candidate to the next phase of the selection process.

When the first interviews have been completed, review your notes and discuss your first impressions with other employees involved in the process. Then, decide who you would like to invite back for a second interview, and let the unsuccessful candidates know they are not right for this particular role.

Step Four: Second Interview + Reference Check

The second interview is used to confirm your impressions of the applicants you believe are well suited to the job. It can also be used to get more information, or to more closely compare two solid candidates.

Make sure you only offer a second interview to those you are considering hiring. If you are on the fence about a candidate, chances are your instincts are right, and bringing them in for a second interview is a waste of their time and yours.

Callbacks

When you call a candidate to invite them to come in for a second interview, remain professional and don't make any allusions to a job offer. If your impression of them changes during the second interview, you do not want to have to go back on something you said. Let them know what you thought of them based on the first interview, and ask if they would be interested in meeting with you a second time.

Give yourself and the candidate at day or two between interviews to reflect on the first interview and prepare for the second.

Interviewer

You may wish to change the person or team of people who conducted the first interview. Usually the second interview is conducted with more senior team members at the table.

Interview Questions

While the second interview is often less structured than the first – a relationship has already begun to be established – you should still prepare a list of questions for the candidate.

These questions should focus on the specific tasks related to the job, and on providing more information about the culture, systems, and values of the company. You can also use the second interview to ask questions you may not have had the chance to in the first interview. As with all interviews be, cognizant of the verbal and non-verbal communication styles of each candidate. Seek help from a local coach if you are not knowledgeable in this area.

Office Tour + Introductions

Once you have determined that you have found the candidate for the job, take them on a tour of your office or business, and introduce them to your staff members. This is a good way gaining an initial understanding of how the candidate might interact with your existing staff members.

Calling References

This is the final – arguably most important – step to make before offering the job to the candidate. You should ask your candidate for at least three employment references, and perhaps one character reference.

Call each reference contact, and explain who you are and why you are calling. Then ask if they have a few moments to answer some questions about the candidate. You will want to find out information about punctuality, professionalism, skills, and their reason for leaving. Cross reference this information with your interview notes to ensure consistency between the candidate and their reference. Be aware that many large companies will only verify employment dates and positions, nothing more.

Determine if a "Trial Period" is Desirable

This can be an effective introduction to your firm and culture. If handled well, it can be quite beneficial for the success of a new employee in current and future iterations. Suggest you do a maximum of 90 days where the technical skills are critical and 30 days where there are simple and well documented processes.

Make sure the expectations are all communicated and success criteria is clearly spelled out and agreed to by both parties.

Step Five: Hire Your Employee

Provided their references are solid, now is the time to make them an offer of employment.

Call the candidate personally to offer them the job. Make sure you congratulate them, and express your enthusiasm in welcoming them into your team. You will also need to follow up your conversation with a letter or email that includes the job offer document or contract.

In the case a candidate declines the job offer, you may wish to do a reference check on your second pick candidate and make them an offer.

Good luck!

Training Your Dream Employees

Once you have landed your dream employees through a rigorous recruitment process, it is essential that you continue to invest in your decision by putting them through a thorough training or onboarding process.

Training is actually an element of recruitment. A new employee's orientation and training sets the tone for their entire employment; this includes their impression of your business, its systems, and respect for its leaders. This has an impact on your ability to retain good people, and avoid unnecessary or redundant recruitment processes.

Too often, businesses rely on junior employees to train new ones without any guidelines or 'curriculum.' New employees are thrown into the deep end without clear expectations or an understanding of 'how things are done around here.'

These elements affect how an employee perceives their own required level of effort or performance. A business that doesn't give much thought to planning, expectations, and preparation will end up showing a new employee that the same lack of attention is expected from them.

Here are some things to ensure you implement when you create your comprehensive training system:

Prior Learning / Existing Knowledge

Acknowledge your new employee's prior learning, and don't overestimate or underestimate their existing knowledge.

Choice of Trainer

Make sure the person or people who will be training the new employee are sufficiently qualified and experienced. If an administrator is leading a salesperson's training and orientation, consider asking another salesperson or more senior team member to assist on specific days or sessions.

Training Materials

Have all the required training materials handy. This includes company manuals, industry guidebooks, common reference materials, work samples and anything else that will aid in the training efforts.

Training Tools

Also ensure you have the tools available to train your new recruit. Will the training be held at their workstation, or another workstation? Do you have all the software you need? All the equipment required? Doing so will ensure the training runs smoothly and the time provided will be used effectively.

Time Investment

Provide more than ample time for training – including time for questions and elaboration. Rushing training benefits no one, including your profits.

Testing Options

Consider including some 'tests' or checks to ensure the new recruit understands each component of the training. Ask the trainer and the trainee to sign-off on each section.

The Big Picture

Each team member's role is part of a larger picture: the company as a whole. Ensure that the trainee understands how their role contributes to the big picture on each level. If they are a junior member of a department, they should understand how their job contributes to the department, as well as how the department contributes to the entire company.

Feedback

The trainee should be able to ask questions and review information at any time – including after the training process. Create an environment that encourages open dialogue and encourages employees to ask questions when they are unsure of a task.

The other common mistake that many companies make is ending training after the first few weeks of a new recruit's employment.

Training is an ongoing process for every single member of your team, and there should be a system or structure in place to ensure that staff training and development happens on a regular basis. This can include cross-training, employee development, and new systems orientation. Regular training not only benefits your staff and improves their performance, but it allows you – the business owner – to:

- Implement new policies + procedures
- Invest in your staff, thereby improving confidence and morale
- Evaluate staff performance at an individual and team level
- Reward staff based on performance improvements
- Provide a regular arena for feedback and discussion, including positive and negative experiences and issues

One-on-One Training + Evaluation

An effective system of ongoing training is weekly, monthly, or quarterly staff reviews. When conducted one-on-one, this provides a forum for regular communication with employees to review performance and identify areas for improvement. A one-on-one environment will encourage more open and honest dialogue than if the session were conducted as part of a team.

As a business owner, these sessions are valuable sources of information and insight into the strengths, weaknesses and motivations of your team.

If you have a large staff, consider pairing junior staff with senior staff and establishing mentorship relationships. This is a powerful way to build the synergy of your team, and frees you up from weekly meetings with each staff member. Instead, each senior staff member can report back to you on the results of their regular training sessions, and you only need to conduct these sessions with your senior staff.

Team Training

Team training events are great team builders, and provide insight into how your team interacts as a whole. These can take the form of "lunch and learns", where senior staff or guest speakers conduct an hour long session with staff members, or more social team building exercises with a less formal program.

Team training exercises will shed light on the leaders and followers in an organization and bring together employees who may work outside of the office. These can be especially helpful if you and your senior staff do not see the team 'in action' on a daily basis.

Keeping Your Dream Employees

Now that you have spent hours of time and potentially hundreds or thousands of dollars recruiting and training your staff, your human resource job is done, right?

I suppose you've done what you've set out to do: get the right people working for you. But what happens when those people get bored? Or stolen by another company?

The final step in the overall recruitment process is employee retention. This includes keeping your employees happy, supporting their development, and giving them incentive to continuously improve their performance.

Environment

The environment you create for your staff has a huge impact on your employee retention rates. This includes the interior design and layout of your office or business, the lighting, plants, and kitchen amenities available. It also includes the culture of the company – what is the general working atmosphere? Are most people loud? Quiet? Is there a buzz or hum to the office space?

Employee engagement is well worth the investment. Note input factors on top and output factors on the bottom of the diagram below:

Spending a little more on comfortable office furniture and amenities like coffee, tea, snacks and social spaces will go a long way toward keeping your employees happy at work.

Recognition, Rewards, and Incentive Programs

Did you know that many employees place more value on positive public recognition for a job well done than they do on salary?

Recognition and rewards are powerful tools when it comes to keeping employees happy. Positive feedback from those in more senior positions has a higher perceived value than a 3-5% salary increase – and it costs the business little to nothing to implement.

Incentive programs are a formalized way of rewarding employees for their achievements and successes. Clear targets and milestones are identified, and when an individual or team reaches those milestones they are rewarded with bonuses or prizes.

Recognition, rewards and incentive programs are an important part of employee retention, as well as team building. They will be discussed in further detail in the Team Building chapter.

Professional Development Programs

Another common reason employees choose to leave their positions is professional development. Many feel they need to move to another company in order to develop their careers or gain more responsibility. They may not necessarily dislike their current role, but become bored or stagnated and believe they have 'done all they can do' at that particular company.

Keeping good people means providing opportunities for growth and advancement within your company. This benefits the company because you can hire from within, and save money and time on recruiting and training new staff. It also benefits your employee and increases their loyalty toward your business.

Professional development programs are an important part of staff retention – but they are also an important part of business growth and development. A company with staff who are always increasing their knowledge and improving their skills will stay on the 'cutting edge' of their industry, and have an advantage over the competition.

Ongoing training and development should be a primary focus for any growing business. Here's why:

- Increases productivity
- Increases staff retention
- Increases workplace safety and morale
- Increases customer service
- Increases sales

Professional development programs should typically focus on the big picture ambitions of the company and its staff members. The longer-term goals and career ambitions are recorded and taken into consideration.

Professional development can be easily worked into your ongoing one-on-one training systems. Keep a folder or binder for each staff member that outlines current role responsibilities, short and long term goals, and areas for improvement, and review it during your weekly or monthly meetings. Identify specific areas for growth, and develop plans of action for that growth.

For example, if your marketing assistant wants to grow into

a marketing coordinator or manager role, and needs to improve her people management skills, consider putting her through a management course or hire a coach to work with her and the team.

Maintaining this program doesn't have to be a time-consuming task. With some simple system tools and a commitment to regularly scheduled meetings, you can have a clear and effective program for your staff.

- Evolving job description document to monitor role responsibilities and tasks
- Regular performance evaluations
- Goal planning worksheets
- Continuing education programs at local business schools
- Regular meetings between staff and supervisors
- Rewards and incentives

10. Profiting from Internet Marketing

"Is your business online? If not, it should be!"

The internet is today's primary consumer research tool. If your business does not have an online presence, it is harder for customers to find and choose your business over the competition. With over 78% of North Americans online, it is no wonder that individuals and businesses in all industries are looking to the internet to enhance their marketing strategies.

Luckily, it has never been easier to establish and maintain a comprehensive online presence. Internet marketing, also referred to as online marketing, online advertising or e-marketing, is the fastest growing medium for marketing.

But it is not just company websites that users are viewing. Blogs, consumer reviews, chat rooms and a variety of social media are growing rapidly in popularity. These supplemental sites often allow input of opinions and perceptions of experiences customers have had with your firm or services, therefore it is in your best interest to be social media aware.

The internet is a very powerful tool for businesses if used strategically and effectively. It can be a cost saving alternative to traditional marketing approaches, and may be the most effective way to communicate with your target consumer.

A major advantage of the internet is that you are always open. Users can access your business 24 hours a day, 7 days a week, and depending on your business and the purpose of the website, visitors can also purchase goods at any time.

Internet Marketing for Everyone

The internet is a great way to create product and brand awareness, develop relationships with consumers and share and exchange information. You can't afford not be taking advantage of online marketing opportunities because your competition is likely already there.

Internet marketing can take on many different forms. By creating maintaining a website for your business, you are reaching out to a new consumer base. You can have full control over the messaging that users are receiving and has a global reach.

Internet marketing can be very cost effective. If you have a strong email database of your customers, an e-newsletter may be cheaper and more effective than post mail. You can deliver time sensitive materials immediately and can update your subscribers instantaneously.

Listed below are the top 16 websites in 2012:

Top 16 Websites (Globally-Alexa - 2012)

1.	Google.com

2.	Facebook.com

3.	You Tube.com

4.	Yahoo.com

5.	Baidu.com

6.	Wikipedia.com

7.	Windows Live

8.	QQ.com

9.   Amazon.com

10.   TaoBao.com

11.   Twitter.com

12.   Blogspot.com

13.   Google! India

14.   LinkedIN.com

15.   Yahoo! Japan

16.   Bing.com

You will notice that many of these websites are search engines. An increasing number of consumers are first researching products, services and companies online, whether it be to compare products, complete a sale, or look for a future employer. When discussing purchases, this has been referred to as "Showrooming".

Most people in the 18-35 age groups obtain all of their information online—including news, weather, product research, etc. Recent data is indicating that 75% or our purchases may be done on line by 2020.

Other age groups are learning the same lessons. While each group is growing in the depth of influence by Social Media, you, as a business owner or manager cannot ignore them.

Internet Marketing Strategies

Internet marketing – like all other elements of your marketing campaign – needs to have clear goals and objectives. Creating brand and product awareness will not happen overnight so it is important to budget accordingly, ensuring there is money set aside for maintenance of the website and analytics.

Be flexible with ideas and options—do your research first, try out different options, then test and measure the results. Metrics and evaluations can be updated almost immediately and should be monitored regularly. By keeping an eye out for what online marketing strategies are working and which are not, it will be easier to create a balanced portfolio of marketing techniques. You might find that in certain geographical areas, certain marketing strategies are more effective than others.

This list is by no means the full extent of options available for marketing online, but it is a good place to start when deciding which options are best suited to your company.

Create a website

The primary use for the internet is information seeking, so you should provide consumers with information about your company first hand. You have more control over your branding and messaging and can also collect visitor information to determine what types of internet users are accessing your website. Keep in mind that a website is not just another brochure; it is dynamic and must be managed appropriately.

You can do this but you must commit to learning the toolsets and add-ons that will be required to remain flexible and dynamic. When you can afford it I highly recommend you hire a good source to handle not only web site construction but also SEO and content management.

Search Engine Optimization (SEO)

Since search engines comprise 50% of the most visited sites globally, you can go through your website to make it more search engine friendly with the aim to increase your organic search listing. An organic search listing refers to listings in search engine results that appear in order or relevance to the entered search terms.

You may wish to repeat key words multiple times throughout your website and write the copy on your site not only with the end reader in mind, but also search engines.

Remember when you design your website; any text that appears in Flash format is not recognized by search engines. If your entire website is built on a Flash platform, then you may have a poor organic search listing.

Price Per Click Advertising

If you find that visitors access your website after searching for it first on a search engine, then it may be beneficial to advertise on these websites and bid on keywords associated with your company.

These advertisements will appear at the top of the page or along the left side of the search results on a search engine. You can have control over the specific geographic area you wish to target, set a monthly budget and have the option on only being charged when a user clicks on your link.

Online Directories

Listing your business in an online directory can be an inexpensive and effective online marketing strategy.

However, you need to be able to distinguish your company from the plethora of competitors that may exist. Likely, you will need to complement this strategy with other brand awareness campaigns.

Online Ads (i.e. banner ads on other websites)

These advertisements can have positive or negative effects based on the reputation and consumer perception of the website on which you are advertising. These ads should be treated similar to print ads you may place in local newspapers or other publications.

Online Videos

With the growing popularity of sites such as YouTube.com, it is evident that people love researching online and being able to find video clips of the information they are seeking. Depending on your small business, you may want to upload informational videos or tutorials about your products or services. If necessary hire a coach to work with you on the initial development of your video process. They should guide you on quality of video & sound, length and setting.

Regular Blogging

Blogging can be a fun and interactive way to communicate with users. A blog is traditionally a website maintained by an individual user that has regular entries, similar to a diary. These entries can be commentary, descriptions of events, pictures, videos, and more. Companies can use blogging as a way to keep users updated on current information and allow them to post comments on your blog. If blogging is something you wish to invest in, make sure that it is regularly updated and monitored.

Top 10 Mistakes to Avoid

1. Failure to measure ROI

Which metrics are you using? Are your visitors actually motivated to purchase or sign up? If the benefits of your online campaign are not greater than the costs incurred, then you may wish to re-evaluate your strategy.

2. Poor Web Design

This can leave a poor impression of your company on the visitor. A poor design could result in frustration on the visitors' part if they are not able to easily find what they went on your site to search for and also does not build trust. If consumers do not trust your company or your website, you will not be able to complete the sale and develop a longer relationship with that customer. You also need to include privacy protection and security when building trust.

This also includes ensuring all information on the website is current and having customer service available if users are experiencing difficulty or cannot find the information they are seeking. This could be as simple as providing a 'Contact Us' email or phone number for support.

3. Becoming locked into an advertising strategy early

Remember your marketing mix when creating a marketing strategy and avoid putting all of your eggs in one basket. Online marketing is a very valuable tool, but depending on your business and your target markets, other marketing campaigns may be the best option for you. Especially if this is your first time making a significant investment into your online sector, you want to remain flexible and able to adapt your strategy based off feedback received by researching and analyzing different options.

4. Acting without researching

Similar to becoming locked into an advertising strategy early, this mistake implies not dutifully testing and researching different online marketing options. For example, if your target consumer is aged 65+ and you are spending all of your marketing efforts into creating a blogging website (where the average ages of bloggers are 18-35), then you are likely not going to have a successful campaign.

5. Assuming more visitors means more sales

You have to go back to your original goals and the purpose of your company. More visitors may not mean more sales if your website is used primarily for information and consumers purchase their products elsewhere. This is also vice versa. You could have an increase in sales without an increase in unique visitors if your current consumer base is very loyal and willing to spend lots of money.

Often people will collect information online about products they wish to purchase because it is easier to compare options, but they purchase in person. Even though shopping online is becoming quite popular, people still prefer to see and feel the physical product before purchasing.

6. Failing to follow up with customers that purchase

Return sales can account for up to 60% of total revenue. It's no wonder that organizations are always trying to maintain loyal customers and may have customer relationship management systems in place. It is easier to get a happy customer to purchase again than it is to get a new customer to purchase once.

7. Failure to incorporate online marketing into the business plan

By ensuring that your online marketing plan is fully integrated and accurately represents your organization's overall goals and objectives, the business plan will be more comprehensive and encompassing.

8. Trying to discover your own best practices

It is very beneficial to use trial and error to determine the best online strategy from your company, but do not be afraid to do your research and learn from what other have already figured out. There will be many cases where someone was in a very similar position as you and they may have some suggestions and secrets that they wish to share. Researching in advance can save a great deal of time and money.

9. Spending too much money too fast

Although it may be cheaper than traditional marketing approaches, internet marketing does have its costs. You have to consider the software and hardware designs, maintenance, distribution, supply chain management, and the time that will be required. You don't want to spend your entire marketing budget all at once.

10. Getting distracted by metrics that are not relevant

As discussed in the following section, there are endless reports and measurables that you can analyze to determine the effectiveness of your campaign. You will need to establish which measurables are actually relevant to your marketing.

Testing and Measuring Online

As with any element of your marketing campaign, you will need to track your results and measure them against your investment. Otherwise, how will you know if your online marketing is successful?

These results - or metrics – need to be recorded and analyzed as to how they impact your overall return on investment.

Some examples of metrics are:

- New account setups
- Conversion rates
- Page stickiness
- Contact us form completion

Due to the popularity in online marketing and the importance of having a strong web presence, companies have demanded more sophisticated tracking tools and metrics for their online activities. It can be very difficult to not only know what to measure, but also HOW to measure.

Thankfully, it is easier than ever to get the information you need with the many types of software and services available, including Google Analytics, which are free and relatively accurate.

8 Metrics to Track

The following are the key measurables to watch for when testing and measuring your internet marketing efforts:

1. Lead Conversions

How many leads has your online presence generated, and of those leads, how many were turned into sales? Ultimately, your campaign needs to have a positive impact on your business.

Regardless of the specific purpose of the campaign – from lead generation and service sign-up, to blog entries – you need to know how many customers are taking the desired action in response to your efforts. Your tracking tool will be able to provide you with this information

2. Lead Generation Spend

If you are not making a profit – or at least breaking even – from your internet marketing efforts, then you need to change your strategy. Redistribute your financial resources and reconsider your motives and objectives for your online campaign.

An easy way to do this analysis is to divide your total spend by conversions. This could also be broken down by product. You could also use tracking tool and view reports on the 'per visit value of every click,' from every type of source. Your sources can include organic/search engine referrals, direct visit (i.e. person typed your web address into their address bar), or email/newsletter.

3. Attention Attraction

You need to keep a close eye on how much attention you are getting on your website. One of the best ways to analyze this would be to compare unique visitors to page views per visit to time on site. How many people are visiting, how many pages they are viewing, what pages they are viewing, and how much time they are spending on the site.

A unique visitor is any one person who visits the website in a given amount of time. For example, if Evelyn visits her online banking website daily for an entire month, over that one month period, she is considered to be one unique visitor (not 30 visitors).

You may also want to incorporate referring source as well – the places online that refer customers to your website.

You'll be able to determine what referring sources offer the 'best' visitors.

4. Top Referrals – Who - Why

Know who is doing the best job of referring clients to your website – and note how they are doing this. Is it the prominence of the link? Positioning? Reputation of the referring company?

Understanding where the majority of your visitors are coming from will allow you focus on those types of sources when you increase your referral sites. They also allow you to gain a better understanding of your online market – and target audience.

5. Current Bounce Rate

The bounce rate is the number of people who visit the homepage of your website, but do not visit other pages. If you have a high bounce rate, you either have all the necessary information on your homepage, or you are not giving your customers a reason to click further.

In Google Analytics, view the 'content' or 'pages' report and view the column stating bounce rate.

6. URL Errors

It is very important to track the errors that visitors receive while trying to access or view your website. For example, if someone links to your website, but makes a spelling error in typing the link, your users will see an error page in their browser, and will not ultimately make it to your website or worse yet wind up at another site that may be totally unrelated or negative image for your business.

You can also receive reports on errors that customer's make when trying to type in your website address in their browser. You may wish to buy the domains with common spelling mistakes, and link those addresses to you true homepage. This will increase overall traffic and potential conversions.

7. Onsite Search Terms

If you have a 'search website' function on your website, it is useful to monitor which terms users are most frequently searching. This can provide valuable insight into the user friendliness of your site and your website's navigation system. This information will be included in the traffic reporting tool.

8. Bailout Rates

If you provide users with the option to purchase something on your website (i.e. shopping cart), then you can track where along the purchasing process people decided not to go through with the sale.

This could be at the first step of receiving the order summary and total, or further when stating shipping options. By obtaining this information, a company can reorganize or revamp their website to make the sales process more fluid and possibly encourage more purchases.

Here are the four main questions you should be asking yourself when evaluating your website presence:

- o Who visits my website?

- o Why do they visit my website?

- o Where do visitors come from?

- o Which pages are viewed?

11. Unlimited Amount of Leads for Your Business?

"Where do your customers come from?"

Most people would probably choose advertising as an answer. Or referrals. Or direct mail campaigns. This may seem true, but it's not really accurate.

Your customers come from leads that have been turned into sales. Each customer goes through a two-step process before they arrive with their wallets open. They have been converted from a member of a target market, to a lead, then to a customer.

So, would it not stand to reason then, that when you advertise or send any marketing material out to your target market, that you're not really trying to generate customers? That instead, you're trying to generate leads.

When you look at your marketing campaign from this perspective, the idea of generating leads as compared to customers seems a lot less daunting. The pressure of closing sales is no longer placed on advertisements or brochures.

From this perspective, the **general purpose of your advertising and marketing efforts is then to generate leads from qualified customers.** Seems easy enough, doesn't it?

Where Are Your Leads Coming From?

If I asked you to tell me the top three ways you generate new sales leads, what would you say?

- Advertising?

- Word of mouth?
- Networking?
- ...don't know?

The first step toward increasing your leads is in understanding how many leads you currently get on a regular basis, as well as where they come from. Otherwise, how will you know when you're getting more phone calls or walk-in customers?

If you don't know where your leads come from, start *today.* Start asking every customer that comes through your door, "how did you hear about us?" or "what brought you in today?" Ask every customer that calls where they found your telephone number, or email address. Then, *record the information for at least an entire week.*

When you're finished, take a look at your spreadsheet and write your top three lead generators here:

1. _____

2. _____

3. _____

From Lead to Customer: Conversion Rates

Leads mean nothing to your business unless you convert them into customers. You could get hundreds of leads from a single advertisement, but unless those leads result in purchases, it's been a largely unsuccessful (and costly) campaign.

The ratio of leads (potential customers) to transactions (actual customers) is called your conversion rate. Simply divide the number of customers who actually purchased something by the number of customers who inquired about your product or service, and multiply by 100.

 # transactions / # leads x 100 = % conversion rate

If, in a given week, I have 879 customers come into my store, and 143 of them purchase something, the formula would look like this:

[143 (customers) / 879 (leads)] x 100 = 16.25% conversion rate

What's Your Conversion Rate?

Based on the formula above, you can see that the higher your conversion rate, the more profitable the business.

Your next step is to determine you own current conversion rate. Add up the number of leads you sourced in the last section, and divide that number into the total transactions that took place in the same week.

Write your conversion rate here: _____.

Quality (or Qualified) Leads

Based on our review of conversion rates, we can see that the number of leads you generate means nothing unless those leads are being converted into customers.

So what affects your ability (and the ability of your team) to turn leads into customers? Do you need to improve your scripts? Your product or service? Find a more competitive edge in the marketplace?

Maybe. But the first step toward increasing conversion rates is to evaluate the leads you are currently generating, and make sure those leads are the right ones.

What are Quality Leads?

Potential customers are potential customers, right? Anyone who walks into your store or picks up the phone to call your business could be convinced to purchase from you, right? Not necessarily, but this is a common assumption most business owners make.

Quality leads are the people who are the most likely to buy your product or service. They are the qualified buyers who comprise your target market. Anyone might walk in off the street to browse a furniture store – regardless of whether or not they are in the market for a new couch or bed frame. This lead is solely interested in browsing, and is not likely to be converted to a customer.

A quality lead would be someone looking for a new kitchen table, and who specifically drove to that same furniture because a friend had raved about the service they received that month. **These are the kinds of leads you need to focus on generating.**

How Do You Get Quality Leads?

- **Know your target market**. Get a handle on where your customers are – the people who are most likely to buy your product or service. Know their age, sex, income, and purchase motivations. From that information you can determine how best to reach your specific audience.

- **Focus on the 80/20 rule.** A common statistic in business is that 80% of your revenue comes from 20% of your customers. These are your star clients, or your ideal clients. These are the clients you should focus your efforts on recruiting. It is also the easiest way to grow your business and your income.
- **Get specific.** Focus not only on who you want to attract, but how you're going to attract them. If you're trying to generate leads from a specific market segment, craft a unique offer to get their attention.
- **Be proactive**. Once you've generated a slew of leads, make sure you have the resources to follow up on them. Be diligent and aggressive, and follow up in a timely manner. You've done to work to get them, now reel them in.

Get More Leads from Your Existing Strategies

Increasing your lead generation doesn't necessarily mean diving in and implementing an expensive array of new marketing strategies. Marketing and customer outreach for the purpose of lead generation can be inexpensive, and bring a high return on investment.

You are likely already implementing many of these strategies. With a little tweaking or refinement, you can easily double your leads, and ensure they are more qualified.

Some popular ways to generate quality leads:

Direct Mail to Your Ideal Customers

Direct mail is one of the fastest and most effective ways to generate leads that will build your business. It's a simple strategy – in fact, you're probably already reaching out to potential clients through direct mail letters with enticing offers.

The secret to doubling your results is to craft your direct mail campaigns specifically for a highly targeted audience of your *ideal* customers.

Your ideal customers are the people who will buy the most of your products or services. They are the customers who will buy from you over and over again, and refer your business to their friends. They are the group of 20% of your clients who make up 80% of your revenue.

Identify your ideal customers

Who are your ideal customers? What is their age, sex, income, location and purchase motivation? Where do they live? How do they spend their money? Be as specific as possible.

Once you have identified who your ideal customers are, you can begin to determine how you can go about reaching them. Will you mail to households or apartment buildings? Families or retirees? Direct mail lists are available for purchase from a wide range of companies, and can be segregated into a variety of demographic and sociographic categories.

Craft a special offer

Create an offer that's too good to refuse – not for your entire target market, but for your ideal customer. How can you cater to their unique needs and wants? What will be irresistible for them?

For example, if you operate a furniture store, your target market is a broad range of people. However, if you are targeting young families, your offer will be much different than one you may craft for empty-nesters.

Court them for their business

Don't stop at a single mail-out. Sometimes people will throw your letter away two or three times before they are motivated to act. Treat your direct mail campaign like a courtship, and understand that it will happen over time.

First send a letter introducing yourself, and your irresistible offer. Then follow up on a monthly basis with additional letters, newsletters, offers, or flyers. Repetition and reinforcement of your presence is how your customer will go from saying, "who is this company" to "I buy from this company."

Advertise for lead generation

Statistics show that nearly 50% of all purchase decisions are motivated by advertising. It can also be a relatively cost effective way of generating leads.

We've already discussed the importance of ensuring your advertisements are purpose-focused. The general purpose of most advertisements is to increase sales – which starts with leads. However ads that are created solely for lead generation – that is, to get the customers to pick up the phone or walk in the store – are a category of their own.

Lead generation ads are simply designed and create a sense of curiosity or mystery. Often, they feature an almost unbelievable offer. Their purpose is not to convince the customer to buy, but to contact the business for more information.

As always, when you are targeting your ideal audience, you'll need to ensure that your ads are placed prominently in publications that audience reads. This doesn't mean you have to fork over the cash for expensive display ads. Inexpensive advertising in e-mail newsletters, classifieds, and the yellow pages are very effective for lead generation.

Here are some tips for lead generation advertising:

Leverage low-cost advertising

Place ads in the yellow pages, classifieds section, e-mail newsletters, and online. If your target audience is technology savvy, consider new forms of advertising like Facebook and Google Adwords.

Spark curiosity

Don't give them all the information they need to make a decision. Ask them to contact you for the full story, or the complete details of the seemingly outrageous offer.

Grab them with a killer headline

Like all advertising, a compelling headline is essential. Focus on the greatest benefits to the customer, or feature an unbelievable offer.

Referrals and host beneficiary relationships

A referral system is one of the most profitable systems you can create in your business. The beauty is once it's set up, it often runs itself.

Customers that come to you through referrals are often your "ideal customers." They are already trusting and willing to buy. This is one of the most cost-effective methods of generating new business, and is often the most profitable. These referral clients will buy more, faster, and refer further business to your company.

Referrals naturally happen without much effort for reputable businesses, but with a proactive referral strategy you'll certainly double or triple your referrals. Sometimes, you just need to ask!

Here are some easy strategies you can begin to implement today:

Referral incentives

Give your customers a reason to refer business to you. Reward them with discounts, gifts, or free service in exchange for a successful referral.

Referral program

Offer new customers a free product or service to get them in the door. Then, at the end of the transaction, give them three more 'coupons' for the same free product or service that they can give to their friends. Do the same with their friends. This ongoing program will bring you more business than you can imagine.

Host-beneficiary relationships

Forge alliances with non-competitive companies who target your ideal customers. Create cross-promotion and cross-referral direct mail campaigns that benefit both businesses.

Lead Management Systems

Once your lead generation strategies are in place, you'll also need a system to manage incoming inquiries. You'll need to ensure you receive enough information from each lead to follow up on at a later date. You'll also need to create a system to organize that information, and track the lead as it is converted into a sale.

Gathering Information from Your Leads

Here is a list of information you should gather from your leads. This list can be customized to the needs of your business, and the type of information you can realistically ask for from your potential customers.

- Company Name
- Name of Contact
- Alternate Contact Person
- Mailing Address
- Phone Number
- Fax Number
- Cell Phone
- Email Address
- Website Address
- Product of Interest
- Other Competitors Engage

Lead List Management Methods:

Once you have gathered information from your lead, you'll need a system to organize their information and keep a detailed contact history.

The simplest way to do this is with a database program, but you can also use a variety of hard copy methods. Whatever method you choose be sure to keep it current, accurate and protected.

Electronic Database Programs

- High level of organization available
- Unlimited space for notes and record-keeping
- Data-entry required

- Examples include: MS Outlook, MS Excel, Maximizer
- Customer Relationship Management Software

Index Cards

- Variety of sizes: 3x5, 4X6 or 5X8
- Basic contact information on one side
- Notes on the other side
- Easy to organize and sort

Rolodex System

- Maintain more contacts than index card system
- Easily organized and compact
- Basic contact information on one side
- Notes on the other side
- Can keep phone conversation and purchase details

Notebook

- Best if leads are managed by a single person
- Lots of room for notes
- Inexpensive
- Difficult to re-organize
- Best for smaller lists

Business Card Organizer

- Limited space for notes
- No data entry required
- Rolodex-style, or clear binder pages
- Best for small businesses – under 100

12. How to Profit through Time Management

"Manage Time Like Money!"

Why did you get into business for yourself? Was it to be your own boss? Choose your own hours? Have more time with the family? Spend more time doing what you love? Chances are, you answered yes to all these questions.

These days, you probably wonder where the time went. Why you spent 12 hours at work and barely make a dent in your to-do list. We already know that time is a key resource for you and your business, but it's also a key resource in your life. Harnessing and leveraging time is the only way to enjoy life, and have a profitable business at the same time.

Most business owners carefully manage their financial and personnel resources, and pay due attention to their performance. Marketing plans and budgets are created, people are hired and fired. What most business owners don't realize is that time – and the time of all employees – requires the same attention and diligent management.

Time will never manage itself. The decision to make a pro-active effort to manage your time must come from you. Once you have committed to taking ownership for your own time management, there are a host of tools available to you. But first, you must understand how much your time is actually worth, and where you are currently spending it.

What is Your Time Worth?

Ever wonder what your time is actually worth? Here's a quick way to figure it out:

Target annual income	A.
Working days in a year	B. 235
Working hours in a day	C. 7
Working hours in a year	D. 1,645
A ÷ D = YOUR HOURLY WORTH (before tax + expenses)	E.

This is a very simple calculation intended to put your time in perspective. In reality, no one is productive for each of the 1,645 hours. Various studies have put actual productivity at anywhere between 25 minutes and four hours per day. Either way, there's a lot of room for improvement.

Let's look at it another way:

Your age	A.
Days in a year	B.
Days spent on earth to date (A x B)	C.
Average life expectancy	D. 78
Total projected days on earth (D x B)	E.
Estimated days left (E – C)	F.

This exercise isn't intended to scare you, but bring your attention to the importance of choosing how you spend each hour you have available. It is a choice! By developing the skills required to manage your time, you will not only have a profitable business, but a rewarding and balanced life.

The Five Culprits of Time Theft

Chances are – if you're like most people – you have no idea where your time goes. You're likely frustrated by the fact that you can spend 10, 12, even 14 hours a day working, and not make a dent in your to-do list, or only bill half of those hours.

When we're too busy and overloaded with work, we often switch into reactive mode. We can't make it to the bottom of the pile, and end up handling issues and making decisions at the last minute. One of the great benefits of choosing to become proactive in time management is that you can become proactive in all other areas of your business. When in proactive mode, you can take steps to grow your business through networking, building programs, and establishing systems.

Before you investigate where your time goes, let's take a look at the top five culprits of modern-day time theft:

1. Your Email

How many times a day do you check your email? Is Outlook or Mail constantly running on your desktop? Email – internal, external, personal and business – clogs up your day like no other communication channel. For many of us, it is possible to spend the entire day writing and responding to emails without even glancing at our inbox. The number of emails sent and received each day by the average person in 2007 was 147. Multiply that by an average of two minutes per message, and you have spent almost five hours one email in a single day. This number is dropping since that time but it has been at the cost of increases in texting, instant messaging and webinars.

2. Your Smartphone, cell phone (Or Blackberry)

Cell phones, smartphones and tablets have created convenience, security, and the luxury of telecommuting They have also created a society that expects to be able to reach you at any moment, or at least receive instant responses to their calls. Your electronic tools not only rob you of your time during the day, but also during the evenings and on weekends when you are with friends or family.

3. Your Open Door Policy

If you make it easy for your staff and associates to interrupt you, they will. Too often, open-door policies are set up by human resource departments to create clear communication channels. Instead, they create a clog of employees lined up at your door seeking immediate answers to non-emergency issues. However, this policy can be used effectively if you have a well communicated policy around your access.

4. Meetings

How many times have you been to a meeting that was scheduled to be an hour, and ended up lasting three? How often do you attend unnecessary meetings? Or meetings that run off-topic? Meetings can be a huge source of wasted time – your valuable time. In a senior management or ownership position, your day may consist of back-to-back meetings, leaving only your evening hours to complete the tasks that should have been done during the day.

5. YOU!

Every person has daily habits that sabotage their ability to work productively and efficiently. Many entrepreneurs and business owners can't separate business hours from leisure hours. Some get caught in a time warp while surfing the internet. Others - mainly overachievers – can become paralyzed by perfectionism or procrastination. Mainly we just don't have the tools to schedule and structure our time in a way that fits with our working style.

Where Does Your Time Go?

So far we've seen that time is a resource that should be as carefully managed as cash, we've figured out what your time is worth, and looked at the top five culprits of time theft. You've committed to taking steps to become a better time manager. What now?

Personal Time Management Research Exercise

The next step is to take a good, (and honest!) look at how you spend your time. Once you understand your patterns and habits, you begin to implement the strategies in this chapter that will make you a better time manager.

Step One: Time Audit

Use the Time Log Worksheet at the back of this chapter, or create a spreadsheet to record how you spend your time for three working days in a row. There are also a number of apps available for your smartphone or tablet that can be utilized. Be honest, and be specific. Include time spent in transit, surfing the web, interacting with clients and colleagues, as well as how your time is spent at home in the evenings. The more information you can record, the easier it will be to analyze your time management skills in step two.

Step Two: Time Categorization

Once you have recorded your time for three days, sit down with all three sheets in front of you and identify the following using different colored markers or highlighters:

Driving, public transportation or other travel

- Eating, including food preparation
- Personal Errands
- Exercise
- Watching TV
- Sleeping, including naps
- Using the computer, personal use only
- Being with family / friends
- Emailing, including checking, reading, and returning messages
- Talking on the phone, including checking and returning messages
- Internal meetings
- External meetings
- Administrative work
- Client work
- Non-client, non-administrative work

Step Three: Time Analysis

Now that you have identified how you have spent your time, go through the worksheets one more time and identify if you have spent enough, too much, or too little time on each main task.

Then, based on your observations, answer the following questions:

1. What patterns do you notice about how you spend your time during the day? (i.e., When are you most productive? Least productive? Most or least interrupted?)

_____

_____

_____

_____

_____

_____

_____

_____

_____

2. Write down the four highest priorities in your life right now. Does your timesheet reflect these priorities?

_____

_____

_____

_____

_____

3. If you have more time, what would you do?

_____

_____

_____

_____

_____

4. If you had less time, what wouldn't you do?

_____

_____

_____

_____

5. Could you remove the items in question four and add the items in question three? Why or why not?

_____

_____

_____

_____

_____

6. Is procrastination a problem for you? How much?

_____

_____

_____

_____

_____

Use Data to Develop Strategies for Profitable Time Management

There are many ways to curb time theft and refine your time management ability. Through a solid understanding of how you currently spend – and waste – time, you can determine which strategies you need to implement to correct unproductive behavior.

Here are 17 ways you can turn less of your time into more money:

1. Set Clear Priorities

The foundation of time management a clear understanding of what your time is best spent on. Once you accept that you can't do everything, you need to decide what needs to be completed now, what can be completed later, and what someone else can complete. Each to-do list you create should be put through this filter, and reorganized so the highest priority items are on top, and the lowest priority items are less visible, or on the bottom.

Once you have established your priorities – which will also naturally reflect the priorities and goals of your business –

stick to them. Just because someone else feels something is of a high priority doesn't mean it holds the same status next to your other tasks.

Prioritization is also helpful in your personal life and leisure time. Your spare time is precious – so make sure are clear on how you would like to spend it. Suggest using Stephen Covey's Quadrants for establishing time priorities:

	Urgent	Not Urgent
Important	**I** ACTIVITIES: Crises Pressing problems Deadline-driven projects	**II** ACTIVITIES: Prevention Relationship building Recreation New opportunities
Not Important	**III** ACTIVITIES: Interruptions Some phone calls Some mail Some meetings Popular activities	**IV** ACTIVITIES: Trivia Some mail Some phone calls Time wasters Pleasure activities

As he points out we should spend 70% of our time in quadrant II. How does your data stack up in this area?

2. Use Your Strengths – Delegate Your Weaknesses

As a business owner, your day naturally consists of tasks you dislike doing. Some are essential – signing checks, reviewing financial statements, and other business maintenance – while others are simply not within your skill set.

If you are a strong public speaker, but struggle with report writing – delegate to a copywriter or editor. If you own a retail store and have no experience in design – outsource your signage. These freelance professionals often cost half as much as you, and take half as long to complete the task. Your time is saved for tasks that use and strengthen your skills effectively, your stress is managed, and ultimately a better product is produced.

3. Delegate, Delegate, Delegate

As a small business owner, the only way you will ever get everything done is by delegating. Delegation is a vital skill that needs to be refined and practiced, and once mastered is the key to profitable time management.

Too often, owners and managers believe that it will be "faster" or "more efficient" to complete the task themselves than to train and monitor someone else. Other times, there are no internal resources to download assignments to.

As a result, the following trends can be seen in many small companies:

- Owners and senior staff are stressed and overworked, while junior staff are underutilized and under capacity.
- Staff members are not given an opportunity to grow and develop in their roles, and may perceive a lack of trust or confidence in their ability. The company loses good people.

- Owners and senior staff are always in a reactive state, instead of a visionary or proactive state.
- Delegation happens at the very last minute, and junior staff has little understanding of either the overall project or expectations for the task.

The easiest way to fix this problem is before it starts. Create a solid team of staff members around you who are well-trained and prepared to support the business. Attract and retain qualified and quality people who can be cross-trained and promoted within the company. Ensure that communication flows throughout the business, so everyone has the product and service knowledge to step in and assist when necessary.

4. Learn to Say "No"

It's easy to fall into the habit of saying yes to everything. You are, after all the business owner, right? No one can complete these tasks as well as you, right? You'll lose that customer if you don't help them with their garage sale, right?

Wrong. The most successful business owners have a keen understanding of how their time is best spent, and *delegate* the remaining responsibilities to trusted others. It's too easy to say yes to every request in the moment, and later feel overwhelmed when it's added to your to do list. You may not ruffle any feathers, but what toll does it take on your stress level? Your workload? Your time is valuable – so protect it!

Remember that if it is too challenging to say no immediately, you can always request some time to think about it. This way, you can evaluate your workload and realistically decide whether or not you can take on a new project. Then, stand by your decision, or assist in bringing in the necessary resources to get it done.

5. Create (and keep!) a Disciplined Schedule

While multi-tasking is a desirable skill, it is also often a time thief. Attempting to do too many things at one time ensures that nothing gets done well. As a business owner, you need   to be able to focus and concentrate on essential projects without interruptions.

The only way to do this is the commit to a strict schedule. Once you understand your work style and concentration patterns, you can allocate periods of the day to specific tasks. This includes personal and leisure time – schedule it, and stick to it.

Schedule time for: list-creation + prioritization, email messages, telephone messages, internal meetings, client meetings, meeting preparation, "me-time", family time, recreation + fitness, daily business tasks, and blocks for focused work.

Remember that there is a training period involved in beginning a new routine – for yourself and those around you. Use your voicemail, out-of-office email message, and a closed door to begin to let people know when you will not be disturbed. Be very disciplined in keeping this creative time available and uncluttered.

6. Make Decisions

The choice to not make a decision is a decision in itself. The most successful business owners have the ability to make good decisions quickly and efficiently, and do not waste time deliberating over simple choices.

In leadership positions, often people are afraid of making the wrong decision or looking foolish if they make a mistake in front of junior staff.   What they don't realize, is that hesitating or avoiding decision making impacts their leadership just as much or more than making the wrong decision.   Not only can being indecisive be personally stressful, but it is also stressful for those around you whose tasks are waiting on your choices.

Remember, you must make the best decision with the information you have, in the time frame you have to make the decision. No one expects you to be a fortune teller – be decisive, make some mistakes, and learn from them.

7. Manage Telephone Interruptions

This is a huge source of time theft that can easily be managed and avoided. If you are available to take phone calls at any time of day, you are setting yourself up to take work home in the evenings.   The phone will always ring when you are focused on an important task, and this is something can easily be avoided.

Figure out when you are most productive. Is it in the morning or the afternoon? Before, during, or after lunch? Once you have identified this time period, set your phone on "do not disturb" or have your calls directed to voicemail. If you do not have a receptionist, a variety of automatic answering systems are available for a nominal fee. To structure your phone time further, let callers know on your voicemail what specific time of day is best to reach you via phone. Then, set that time aside to receive and return phone calls.

8. Keep Your Work Environment Organized

Have you ever tried to make dinner in a messy kitchen? More of your time is spent looking for and cleaning dishes and tools than actually spent cooking the meal.

The same goes for your work environment. If your desk and office is in a constant state of chaos, then you mind will be too. In fact, some studies have revealed that the average senior business leader spends nearly four weeks each year navigating through messy or cluttered desks, looking for lost information. Does that sound like productive time to you?

Once you make the initial clean sweep, it's easy to maintain order in the chaos:

- Tidy your desk at the beginning and end of each day. Attach pertinent documents to your to do list, or have clear and organized folders for loose papers.
- Organize your supplies drawer so you have easy access to stationery like pens, post-it notes, staplers and highlighters. Every minute counts!
- Only have the documents and files you are working on, on your desk. The rest should be neatly filed on a side table for later retrieval.
- Keep personal items (like photos or memorabilia) out of your primary line of vision. These can be distracting and encourage daydreaming.

As for your office or store, there are many ways to make its layout more conducive to effective time management. Try:

- Minimizing the distance between the reception desk and electronics like photocopies and fax machines.

- Keep a clear line of sight between your office and the most productive area of your business, so you are aware of what is happening amongst your staff.
- Organize shelves and filling cabinets so files are not only easily accessed, but out of sight when not being used. Consider putting sliding doors or cabinets in storage areas, and remember that the floor is not a storage cabinet.

9. Keep Your Filing System Organized

If your data isn't organized properly, you will waste hundreds of hours searching for documents you need on a regular basis. This includes both electronic and hard copy files; they need to be organized and up to date.

Customer databases and enquiry records are worth their weight in gold. They are an asset of the business. You can't afford to get behind when updating this information, or poorly store it for later retrieval. There are many easy to use software programs that will manage and organize customer databases for you; it doesn't need to be a time consuming or tedious exercise.

A simple way to manage information is to keep it in short, medium, and long term files for both hard and electronic copies. Create shortcuts on your desktop for folders or files you constantly access. Have short-term files available on your desk, medium-term files available within an arm's reach, and long-term files stored in cabinets.

10. Clearly Communicate – Never Assume

One of the biggest issues for time management in business – and likely the world – is miscommunication or lack of communication. This is a dangerous issue that can cripple any business, including yours. Establishing and enforcing clear policies on things like accurate note taking, task assignments, and phone messages will ensure your staff understand the importance of clear and accurate communication.

The easiest habit to start to curb miscommunication is simple: write everything down. Carry a notepad or use your smartphone or tablet, and jot down key points, figures, agreements and deadlines. Don't assume you'll remember later – you have at least a hundred other things to remember.

Some other simple strategies are:

- Return all necessary communications promptly, including email, letters, faxes and phone calls
- Repeat back phone messages, phone numbers and other figures to confirm you recorded the information correctly.
- Record appointments in your smartphone, tablet or agenda the moment you make them. Otherwise, you will forget.
- Double check and confirm everything – addresses, phone numbers, meeting locations and times.
- Maintain accurate customer contact logs with dates, times, and phone numbers.
- Create and post checklists in your store or office for routine operations procedures.
- Announce any changes to the policies and procedures manual immediately.

11. Stop Duplicating Efforts

This is a key element of time management that is closely related to effective communication. Studies have continually shown that many businesses often duplicate and triplicate efforts that need only be completed once.

When you have clear systems and procedures in place, your staff will not need to "reinvent the wheel" each time the task needs to be completed. Meeting minutes and individual task assignments will ensure everyone is on the same page and understands their personal responsibilities.

Simple examples of this include re-reading your to-do list each hour to determine what the next important item is. If your list is already structured by priority, this is a needless task. If two staff members are working on similar projects, but unaware of the other, the work will not only be inconsistent, but the efforts will be duplicated. These are easy problems to fix, once they have been identified and communicated.

12. Say Goodbye to Procrastination & Perfectionism

Procrastination is something we all face at one time or another – and likely have since our school days. However, given the pace that the world operates at today, you will only fall behind your competitor if you allow procrastination to rule your day. So how you do avoid it? It's simple. Stop, and just get started, no matter how boring, tedious, or painful the project may be. Reward yourself by crossing each step off your to-do list.

Many small business owners also fall victim to perfectionism, which can be paralyzing. The fear that there isn't enough time or resources to "get it perfect" will sometimes stop you dead in your tracks. Perfectionism can also hinder your ability to delegate and say no to tasks you believe no one else can complete "better". Do the best you can with the time and resources you have – and just get started.

13. Plan Your Work, Work Your Plan

Have you ever placed an advertisement on the fly because it was "cheaper", "faster", or "more urgent" than creating a marketing plan? Do you and your staff have a clear idea of where your business is headed over the next six to 12 months, or five years?

Many studies show that less than 10% of small businesses have up to date marketing and business plans, as compared to the majority of large corporations and public companies, which have both. Having a plan is step one, not the destination.

Marketing and business plans take time and effort to create – but they work, and pay off in spades. They also save you time and money as compared to a haphazard or fly-by-the-seat-of-your-pants strategy. With a marketing plan in place, you will have an idea of how many ads you will be placing in a year, which will earn you a volume discount. Your marketing materials will complement each other, and deliver the same message to the same target audience. Designers will charge less for a package of collateral than for individual collateral items.

A business plan will provide you with a guide to reference when making decisions. You can repeatedly ask if the endeavor at hand will contribute to your overall vision, or just seems like a good idea or price.

Remember that planning includes both short and long-term time frames, and applies to both your daily to-do list, and your marketing budget. It provides you with a means to measure your progress, assists in identifying priorities, and helps to manage your time. Make sure the plans are communicated to everyone involved so there is buy-in to ensure success.

14. Avoid Needless, Impromptu & Unstructured Meetings

This may seem like a time theft issue that is out of your control, but it's not. You are in control of your own time, and through strict scheduling can establish a structure for internal and external meetings that everyone around you can work within.

Minimize impromptu internal meetings by letting your staff know when you're available for a "quick chat" and when you are not. If it is important, ask them to schedule a time to meet with you that works with both of your schedules. This not only saves you time, but encourages staff to find solutions to their own issues, and only approach you with more urgent or challenging matters.

You can't avoid having meetings, but you can avoid having unstructured meetings. Ask for or create an agenda for each meeting you attend, with a clear objective and an amount of time allocated to each item. Set a start and stop time for each meeting and work to make this a reality. This will keep your meetings focused and on task. However, if a meeting does run late, give yourself a reasonable buffer, and politely leave for your next appointment. You can always follow up with a colleague to catch-up on the pertinent items you may have missed.

15. Establish Clear Policies & Procedures

A clear policy and procedures manual is like a marketing or business plan – it takes time to create, but ultimately saves everyone in your company time, money and effort. A step-by-step guide to "the way we do things here" is an invaluable resource for your existing and new staff, and provides clear expectations for how you like things done.

Too many businesses make up policies and procedures on the fly – creating dangerous scenarios where mistakes are made and expectations are not clear. Some items that should be included in a comprehensive policy and procedures manual include:

- Recruitment
- Customer relations
- Customer inquiries
- Customer complaints
- Social Media utilization
- Internet use within the work network
- Returns
- Exchanges
- Late Payments
- Salary structure
- Bonus structure
- Employee review
- Theft
- Harassment

16. Keep the Right Set of Tools

The equipment your business needs to operate (and grow!) effectively should always be on hand, or easily contracted out. This is specific to each company, and closely related to costs – including the cost of your time.

Whether you are a high-tech business or local retailer, knowledge of the latest advancements in technology will increase your efficiency. It will help you stay on top of the competitor, maintain your position as an expert, and perhaps provide an easier way of getting things done.

Always ask yourself if these purchases are essential to your business –could perhaps make these purchases from a second hand dealer to minimize cost? Is it more cost effective to outsource or sub-contract the tasks to someone with access to this equipment, or to buy the equipment yourself?

If your business relies on tools and technology for daily tasks (such as the trades' profession) then obtaining the best quality you can afford is crucial.

17. Maintain Your Equipment

This may seem obvious, but you'll understand the importance if your network server has ever crashed, or point of sale system has malfunctioned. Your business can be slowed to a stand-still if your equipment is not in good working order. Of course there are instances that can't be predicted, but regular maintenance of your essential equipment will reduce these occurrences and help to anticipate when old equipment needs to be repaired or replaced.

This includes updating software packages, operating systems, mechanical equipment, office equipment and even the phone system. Make this a proactive task rather than reactive.

For example, take the case of a restaurant owner who knows they have an issue with a freezer but put off having it repaired fully or replacing the item. Murphy's Law will dictate that it will break down again, at the most inopportune time, for example, in the middle of the night. He is risking spoilage and lack of food to fill orders when he reopens. They may also waste a lot of man hours moving from one freezer to another to minimize the spoilage. These events could cost hundreds, even thousands of dollars to mitigate. By having a proactive maintenance plan, internal-external or both, he could have avoided many of the unexpected costs.

Personal Time Management Strategy

Choose the top five tips from this chapter that you think will help you the most, given your personal time management research. Write them below, with three corresponding actions that you will start tomorrow. For example, if you are going to set a strict schedule, three actions might be to establish the schedule, communicate it to your staff, and re-record your voicemail message.

1. _____

    a._____

    b._____

    c._____

2._____

    a._____

    b._____

    c._____

3._____

a._____

b._____

c._____

4._____

a._____

b._____

c._____

5._____

a._____

b._____

c._____

Timesheet | Day One

Time slot	Activities	More/Less/ Enough time?
7:00 – 7:30		
7:30 – 8:00		
8:00 – 8:30		
8:30 – 9:00		
9:00 – 9:30		
10:00 – 10:30		
10:30 – 11:00		
11:00 – 11:30		
11:30 – 12:00		
12:00 – 12:30		
12:30 – 1:00		
1:00 – 1:30		
1:30 – 2:00		
2:00 – 2:30		
2:30 – 3:00		
3:00 – 3:30		
3:30 – 4:00		
4:00 – 4:30		
4:30 – 5:00		
5:00 – 5:30		

Timesheet | Day Two

Time slot	Activities	More/Less/ Enough time?
7:00 – 7:30		
7:30 – 8:00		
8:00 – 8:30		
8:30 – 9:00		
9:00 – 9:30		
10:00 – 10:30		
10:30 – 11:00		
11:00 – 11:30		
11:30 – 12:00		
12:00 – 12:30		
12:30 – 1:00		
1:00 – 1:30		
1:30 – 2:00		
2:00 – 2:30		
2:30 – 3:00		
3:00 – 3:30		
3:30 – 4:00		
4:00 – 4:30		
4:30 – 5:00		
5:00 – 5:30		

Timesheet | Day Three

Times lot	Activities	More/Less/ Enough time?
7:00 – 7:30		
7:30 – 8:00		
8:00 – 8:30		
8:30 – 9:00		
9:00 – 9:30		
10:00 – 10:30		
10:30 – 11:00		
11:00 – 11:30		
11:30 – 12:00		
12:00 – 12:30		
12:30 – 1:00		
1:00 – 1:30		
1:30 – 2:00		
2:00 – 2:30		
2:30 – 3:00		
3:00 – 3:30		
3:30 – 4:00		
4:00 – 4:30		
4:30 – 5:00		
5:00 – 5:30		

Daily To-Do List | Business

Task	Priority (1-10)	Deadline?	Delegation?

Weekly To-Do List | Personal

Task	Priority (1-10)	Deadline?	Delegation?

So What Do You Do From Here?

"Now you've finished this book, what do you do NEXT?"

Very Important: Take Action! If you're already an accomplished business owner and earning in excess of $250,000.00 per year (rich according to the Federal Government), use this book as a guide to enhance the speed of your business success. If you are not as accomplished as you would like to be then the smartest thing to do is:

A) **Get out of your comfort zone:** If you are locked in that area of your life called the comfort zone, you will not extend yourself with learning; idea generation or worse yet feel powerless. Be willing to try new ideas and thoughts, release the "We've Done It that Way Before "🗆attitude.

B) **Commit to Personal Growth, (Growth = Change):** Change can be exciting and exhilarating or it can be painful and foreboding, the choice and control is yours but you have to act.

C) **Develop a leadership navigation plan:** Every idea or thought you generate as a result of reading should be written down, evaluated against your current environment, then intentionally and strategically implemented or adapted to your particular style.

D) **Connect with Your Plan:** Open, honest, transparent communications and connection will help your plan become more effective and easier to implement. Bounce it off of your inner circle of friends, family members, and other business leaders you trust. I also suggest you include your current employees; they will embrace your trust in them and rapidly become more engaged.

Concentrate on strategies to **LEARN** then the **EARN** will follow! If you are serious about taking the next step then go to work on yourself first; study other business successes, understand marketing strategies, hire a coach and become a sponge for new (proven) material. The amazing thing about the game of business is that when you put proven processes to work and discipline yourself and your team to follow them, an abundance of success will follow. The biggest mistake is to start a process and then fallback into your old habits after a short time.

Above all, get the knowledge you need before you step onto the field. However, don't get locked into analysis paralysis. Think about it; if you were going to challenge Michael Jordan to a game of H O R S E for money, wouldn't it make sense to learn the game and practice before you stepped on the court to play him? It is amazing to me how many new small business people start the game of business against seasoned professionals (the competition), without first developing the necessary knowledge to be successful. Then they fail and blame the market, the economy, their location, etc.

If you have a business and have not yet managed to start the creation of wealth and systems that allow you to take time off, build retirement accounts or pay for your children's college, then learn and master the steps outlined in my book. I am a huge advocate of education and mentorships. Get the right information, find someone that knows how to walk you through them and watch your quality of life take new shape.

If you would like to see more on business coaching, team building frameworks and personal assessment packages check at http://transformativeleadership.us website.

www.ingramcontent.com/pod-product-compliance
Lightning Source LLC
Chambersburg PA
CBHW051653170526
45167CB00001B/450